USS CONSTI

*A Short History
of the Last All-Sail Warship
Built by the U.S. Navy*

GLENN F. WILLIAMS

DEDICATION

To my father, Franklin Ezra Williams,

who planted in me the love of history;

and to my mother,

Marie Kaminski Williams Rohrbach,

who nurtured it.

The Donning Company Publishers
184 Business Park Drive, Suite 106
Virginia Beach, VA 23462

Steve Mull, General Manager
B. L. Walton Jr., Project Director
Dawn V. Kofroth, Assistant General Manager
Sally Clarke Davis, Editor
Lori Wiley, Designer
John Harrell, Imaging Artist
Scott Rule, Senior Marketing Coordinator
Patricia Peterson, Marketing Coordinator

Library of Congress Cataloging-in-Publication Data
Available upon request
Printed in the United States of America

CONTENTS

47

A.Robertson Pinx. C.Tiebout Sculp.

COMMODORE TRUXTON,
OF THE
NAVY OF THE UNITED STATES.

New York Published by A.Robertson N.º 79 Liberty Str.ª & C.Tiebout N.º 28 Gold Street.
Novem.ª 20.ª 1799.

Commodore Thomas Truxtun.

CHAPTER 1

THE GLORIOUS NAMESAKE

WHEN PRESIDENT GEORGE WASHINGTON SIGNED THE ACT OF Congress authorizing the acquisition of six warships to protect American commerce against the attacks of the Barbary States into law on 27 March 1794, it signaled the reestablishment of the U.S. Navy. Hotly debated, the Act had passed by only two votes! The six ships, initially designated alphabetically "A" through "F," would eventually be named *United States*, *Constitution*, *President*, *Chesapeake*, *Constellation*, and *Congress*, respectively. Vessels A, B, and C were to be "first-class" frigates rated at 44 guns each, while D, E, and F were "second-class" frigates rated at 36. President Washington, insisting that the benefits from building the ships should be distributed among several states, selected six port cities where they would be built: A at Philadelphia, B at Boston, C at New York, D at Norfolk, E at Baltimore, and F at Portsmouth (New Hampshire).[1]

The United States Congress did not pass an act forming the Navy Department until 30 April 1798, therefore, initial construction began under the direction of the War Department (today's Department of the Army). Secretary of War Henry Knox appointed Philadelphia ship designer Joshua Humphreys as Naval Constructor to design the vessels. The thirty-six-gun frigate "E" was assigned to Baltimore, and in June 1794, Thomas Truxtun, a veteran privateer captain of the War for Independence, was appointed a Captain in the new U.S. Navy to command the ship. Together with Naval Constructor David Stodder of Baltimore, he was ordered to superintend construction of the frigate in the shipyard of Samuel and Joseph Sterrett, "reputable builders of merchant vessels," at Harris Creek. In 1795, the ship's keel was laid.[2]

When the new Republic signed a peace treaty with the Dey of Algiers in 1795, work on all six vessels was suspended. Congress passed "An Act to Provide a Naval Armament" on 20 April 1796, however, which authorized completion of the three whose construction was most advanced: 44-gun *United States* and *Constitution*, and 36-gun *Constellation*. While attempting to launch *United States* on 10 May 1797, the ship went down the ways too early and too fast. She sustained hull damage that required significant repair, and delayed another launching by several months. *Constellation* was successfully launched on 7 September 1797, followed by *Constitution* on 21 October. The Baltimore-built frigate was the first of the new ships to be commissioned in the United States Navy. Carrying 38 guns, although originally designed for 36, and displacing 1,265 tons with a 164 foot length and 40 foot, 6 inch beam, *Constellation* combined the firepower of a standard frigate with the celerity of a Baltimore Clipper, built at a cost of $314,212.[3]

In 1798, the United States became involved in an undeclared naval conflict with France known as the "Quasi War." This was brought about by the French Republic's interference with American maritime commerce, and not respecting U.S. neutrality in its war with Great Britain. Under Truxtun's command, *Constellation* convoyed American merchant ships between the Chesapeake Bay and the Caribbean Sea on her first two cruises from June to October 1798. Owing to Truxtun's leadership, *Constellation*'s crew established traditions of discipline and organization in the U.S. Navy that still apply. Truxtun's insistence on drill made *Constellation's* crew formidable with their twenty-eight 24-pounder long guns (fourteen on each side) on her gun deck, and ten 12-pounder long guns on her spar, or upper, deck.[4]

In December 1798, Truxtun was ordered to take *Constellation* to join the U.S. West India Squadron, then patrolling between St. Kitts and Puerto Rico, to protect American commerce. *Constellation* encountered the 40-gun French frigate *L'Insurgente* off the island of Nevis on 9 February 1799. For both *Constellation* and the new U.S. Navy, its was baptism by fire. After failing to damage *Constellation's* rigging, *Insurgente* closed to grapple. In a close fight, the two ships exchanged broadsides of cannon fire. The French, with a view to taking the American vessel as a prize, aimed their guns at the masts and rigging in an attempt to immobilize their foe. American tactics, like those of the British, preferred to pound the enemy ship's hull into a pulp and her crew into submission.[5]

U.S. Frigate *Constellation* and Sloop-of-War *Baltimore* escorting an American convoy during the Quasi War in 1798. (By Arthur Disney)

After trading broadsides at close range, with American gunfire having greater effect, Truxtun maneuvered *Constellation* ahead and crossed the Frenchman's bow. As every gun on the starboard side came to bear, it fired down the length of *L'Insurgente* causing more damage. Looking for an opportunity to take advantage of his 409 to 309 numerical superiority in crew, French Captain Barreaut ordered his men on deck to prepare to board *Constellation.* Truxtun detected the maneuver, and drew away firing another devastating broadside. He then crossed the bow again, and loosed yet another round of raking fire. Finally, after little more than an hour, Barreaut struck *L'Insurgente's* colors in surrender. The Americans suffered five killed and wounded, while the French suffered at least seventy casualties.

In succeeding months, *Constellation* continued cruising West Indian waters. She encountered and captured the French privateers *Diligent* and *Union* before returning to the United States for repair and refitting. While in the shipyard, *Constellation* was rearmed, and set sail again carrying twenty-eight 18-pounder long guns on the gun deck and ten 24-pounder carronades on the spar deck.[6]

After a brief and uneventful patrol under Captain Samuel Barron, *Constellation* was again placed under the command of Truxtun, who now held the rank of Commodore. In December 1799, he took the ship to the West Indies once more. Off the French base on the island of Guadeloupe, *Constellation* sighted the 52-gun frigate *La Vengeance* on 1 February 1800. In a furious five-hour slugging match that lasted from about 8 p.m. until 1 a.m. the next morning, *Constellation* suffered fourteen dead and twenty-five wounded from her crew of 320 officers and men. *La Vengeance*, a total wreck in danger of sinking, had twice struck her colors. When *Constellation* became disabled by the loss of her mainmast and was unable to pursue, the French frigate made good her escape in the darkness. One witness later reported that *La Vengeance* arrived at Curacao completely dismasted with sixty dead and over one hundred wounded from among the crew of five hundred officers and men, plus sixty soldiers being transported on board. Captain F. M. Pitot told the French naval board inquiring on the loss of his ship that he had engaged a ship-of-the-line: a tribute to the gunnery of the American sailors. For his command of *Constellation* in the battle, Congress awarded Truxtun a gold medal.[7]

Following repairs at Norfolk, Captain Alexander Murray assumed command, and by the middle of May, *Constellation* was heading back to the Caribbean. With her crew itching for a rematch that would finish *La Vengeance*, *Constellation* took up station near Guadeloupe. The diplomats soon negotiated an end to the fighting, but not before *Constellation* recaptured three American merchantmen that had been taken by French privateers. The frigate *Constellation* was the hero ship of the undeclared Quasi War.

With Captain Murray still in command, *Constellation* joined the Mediterranean Squadron and participated in the campaigns against the Barbary States from 1802 to 1805. After sailing home to Washington, D.C. in 1803, she returned to the Mediterranean in 1804 under the command of Captain Hugh G. Campbell. *Constellation* took part in the successful naval operations against the Barbary States that enabled American emissaries to work out a treaty in which the United States flag on merchant ships would be respected. After the treaty was signed, the fleet sailed for home. The administration of President Thomas Jefferson, as well as his successor James Madison, saw little further need for maintaining a strong deep-water navy. On returning to American waters, *Constellation,* and much of the fleet, was put "in ordinary" (a condition similar to a steel ship being "mothballed") at the Washington Navy Yard with only a small caretaker crew.[8]

By the early months of 1812, British interference with American merchant shipping, and the "War Hawks'" desire to expand U.S. national borders into areas controlled by Great Britain and her Indian allies were leading to war. With hostilities imminent, Congress directed the immediate repair and commissioning of *Constellation* and two other frigates on 30 March. *Constellation* was also rearmed with 44 guns: twenty-four 18-pounder and two 32-pounder long guns, and eighteen 32-pounder carronades. But when war was declared against Great Britain on 18 June, *Constellation* still required six months of preparation. With Captain Charles Stewart in command, *Constellation* finally headed for the Atlantic in January 1813, but was unable to make ocean waters before an imposing British fleet blockaded the entrance of Chesapeake Bay.

Kedging up the Elizabeth River, *Constellation* anchored abreast of Craney Island to assist the Army defending the important port city of Norfolk, Virginia. On 7 June 1813, Stewart was ordered to take command of the frigate *Constitution*, and was replaced by Master Commandant Joseph Tarbell. With some of her sailors and marines manning shore batteries on the island, and the rest of the crew fighting from the ship on 20 June, *Constellation* defeated a British amphibious assault by 700 seamen, marines, and soldiers in fifteen boats and supported by a number of warships. Shortly after Tarbell's promotion to Captain in July and subsequent transfer, Captain Charles Gordon took command of the frigate on 28 August 1813. Moving their campaign up the Chesapeake, the British kept a naval force in the area for the remainder of the war to prevent *Constellation* from getting to sea.[9]

During the United States' preoccupation with the war against Britain, the Barbary

Medal awarded to Thomas Truxtun after *Constellation*'s battle with *La Vengeance.*

States had resumed their depredations against American shipping. Soon after ratification of the Treaty of Ghent that ended the War of 1812, *Constellation* was again in the Mediterranean. On 17 June 1815, *Constellation* was the first of four American ships that engaged the 46-gun Algerian frigate *Mashuda* and forced her surrender. The American squadron then stood by to help the diplomats exact treaties from leaders of the three Barbary States. By August, when most of the squadron returned home, *Constellation* remained on station with a small force to ensure the pledges were honored. After Captain Gordon died at Messina, he was replaced by Captain William M. Crane. The ship returned to Hampton Roads on 26 December 1817.[10]

Except for brief periods of repair, the U.S. Frigate *Constellation* remained in active service through 1845. During the 1820s and 30s, she took part in operations to eradicate the last of the Caribbean Sea pirates, interdict the importation of slaves to the United States, protect American interests during the wars of independence in South America, and supported the Army during the Seminole War. In the 1840s *Constellation* circumnavigated the globe as the flagship of the East Indies Squadron under Captain, later Commodore, Lawrence Kearney. The squadron protected American interests during the Opium Wars in China, and was on hand when Commodore Kearney negotiated the foundations for trade agreements in Chinese ports. Before returning to the United States, *Constellation* showed the flag in the Hawaiian Islands to deter a British or French takeover of the chain. After rounding Cape Horn in February, *Constellation* arrived at Hampton Roads on 1 May 1844 having logged more than 58,000 nautical miles. The ship was placed in ordinary at the Gosport Navy Yard, near Portsmouth, Virginia in 1845, and remained there for eight years.[11]

By 1853, the frigate *Constellation* was in poor condition. An extensive survey reported the old ship had "hogged," or sagged with her bow and stern lower in the water than at amidships, and was twisted and deteriorated beyond repair. On 22 February 1853 the old ship was moved to the North Slip, and the following day at 1 p.m., she was hauled out of the water. On 15 May work crews began dismantling the frigate and cutting up the timbers. Hundreds of pounds of copper, brass, and iron pieces that could be melted for scrap, and almost 23,000 pounds of cast pig-iron ballast were turned in to the storekeeper. When the Yard Commandant wrote to the Secretary of the Navy requesting permission to auction off the usable timbers, the frigate *Constellation* existed no more.[12]

Frigate *Constellation* off Port Mahon circa 1815.

John Lenthall, Chief of the Bureau of Construction, USN, 1853–1871, and designer of the Sloop-of-War *Constellation*. (U.S. Naval Historical Center)

CHAPTER 2

THE SAME VENERABLE NAME

As the old frigate *Constellation* lay in ordinary at the Gosport Navy Yard from 1845 to 1853, the navies of the world were changing. With the introduction of naval guns capable of firing exploding shells and the widespread adoption of steam propulsion, the future of frigates and ships-of-the-line, especially those powered only by sail, around which most fleets had once been built, was limited.

During the War of 1812, the British blockade of American ports severely crippled the ability of the U.S. Navy to build new and repair existing warships required for fighting a major war at sea. To insure the Navy's preparedness in future conflicts, Congress passed the Act of 29 April 1816, which provided for the annual expenditure of $1,000,000 per year for eight consecutive years for the purchase of timber to build warships. These ships were to be kept on the stocks ready for launching in the event of national emergency. Congress renewed the "Act for the Gradual Improvement of the Navy" on 3 March 1827, and authorized the president to use $500,000 per year for six consecutive years to procure substantial supplies of live oak to be stockpiled at shipyards. Although Congress made it known that no new ships needed to be built immediately, the "Gradual Increase Act" was renewed again in 1833 for six more years. By 1840, continued funding for the same purpose was included in the annual naval appropriations with language that permitted the acquisition of other timbers and guns, as well as the repair and armament of ships. The Navy called it the "Gradual Increase, Repairs, Etc." appropriation.[1]

Under provisions of the legislation, the Navy not only stockpiled the wood, but prepared sets of components for each type of vessel: ships-of-the-line, frigates, sloops-of-war, steamers, and brigs. Pre-cut generic frames, keels, keelsons, and beams were stored in sheds or submerged in timber ponds until needed. As the legislation prevented the selling of surplus components, it became standard practice to use the yards' spare structural timbers for repair, as well as new construction of ships when it was more cost effective to replace vessels in extremely poor condition. In fact, the use of pieces from stockpile was seen as an ideal method of drawing down the supply to more economic levels, and became standard Navy practice.[2]

The Navy was free to use the stockpiles of wood, and cover its labor costs from the Gradual Increase appropriation. There was little congressional interest in increasing the size of the fleet in 1852, so the Navy sought to improve the quality of the ships it had. The Navy chose, therefore, to substitute a new sloop-of-war *Constellation* for the old, now obsolete frigate of the same name. Adding an auxiliary steam engine was considered, but the purchase of boilers and engines would have required separate Congressional funding, and a number of new steamers had already been built under specific appropriations. The Navy opted for a ship of sail-only design, capable of good speed and long cruising range. A reliable all-sail sloop-of-war was relatively inexpensive to operate, and a competitive alternative to coal guzzling steamers for distant cruising. It represented a concession to economics in an era of austere military budgets.[3]

John Lenthall, who served as Chief of the U.S. Navy Bureau of Construction and Repair from 1853 to 1871, prepared the plans for the new *Constellation*, and probably took the sizes and shapes of the timbers in the Gosport stockpile into consideration. Representing the best all-sail design, *Constellation* was the largest U.S. Navy sloop-of-war to that date. In May 1853, workers at Gosport began gathering the timbers for the new ship.[4]

Work began under the supervision of Naval Constructor Edward H. Delano. After Delano's transfer to the Charlestown Navy Yard, the project came under the supervision of Constructor Samuel T. Hartt, and Captain John L. Porter, the Master Ship Builder.[5] The keel of the sloop-of-war *Constellation* was laid out in Shiphouse B, within walking distance from where the remains of frigate *Constellation* were being disassembled, on 25 June 1853. Reading like both an obituary and a birth announcement, an article appearing in *The Daily Southern Argus* on 11 July 1853 said:

> The old time-worn and time-honored frigate of historical memory has been literally torn to pieces, preparatory to the building of the new *Constellation*. Hundreds of men are employed directly or indirectly upon her massive keel, which has been placed in one of the ship houses. She will be finished with all possible dispatch. Her name itself is a source of pride to every American sailor, and no doubt will be cherished and esteemed by all lovers of American freedom.[6]

Larger than most other ships of her class, being closer in size to a second-class frigate than a first-class sloop-of-war, and carrying a battery of the heavy guns becoming standard on U.S. warships, *Constellation* was sometimes referred to as a "corvette."

On Saturday 26 August 1854, at twenty minutes before noon, before thousands of cheering spectators, "the United States Ship *Constellation* slid gracefully forth from the gigantic shiphouse in which she was constructed, and floated out majestically upon the deep waters of our spacious harbor."[7] Described as a "beautiful piece of naval architecture," the new *Constellation* measured her extreme (Knighthead to Taffrail) length as 186 feet, with a length between perpendiculars of 176 feet, and a molded beam of 41 feet.[8] Materials included live oak for frames, stem, knees, breasthooks, and mooring bitts; white oak for hull planking, knees, keel, sternpost, and keelson posts; yellow pine for deck beams, ceiling, and decking; white pine for joiner bulkheads and heavy spars; spruce for light spars; and locust for trunnels.[9]

The corvette *Constellation* was to be a formidable man-of-war. Although her hull was pierced for twenty-four gun ports on the gun deck, there would only be twenty cannons arranged for broadside firing. Her main armament consisted of sixteen 8-inch naval chambered shell guns, eight each on the port and starboard sides of the gun deck. These shell guns were a new type of shipboard armament being adopted throughout the navy, based on the innovative design of French artillery officer Henri Paixhans. They were the size of 68-pounder solid shot firing guns, but hurled exploding shells that were so destructive to wooden ships. *Constellation* also carried four 32-pounder solid shot long guns on the gun deck: one on either end of the 8-inch battery on both sides. In addition, two 10-inch shell guns were located on the spar deck, one each at the forecastle and stern, on pivot mounts.[10]

For ship's boats, *Constellation* carried one launch armed with a 12-pounder boat howitzer, and five cutters. Drinking water for the crew was stored in forty-eight iron tanks capable of holding a total of 28,000 gallons. For stability, sixty-one long tons of iron ballast were stored in the hold. To moor the ship, she held 150 fathoms, or about 900 feet, of 1-13/16 inch iron chain for four anchors, each of which weighed approximately 6,000 pounds.[11]

In June 1855, as the new ship with the venerable old name was being made ready to join the fleet, Secretary of the Navy John C. Dobbin notified Lenthall that *Constellation* was urgently needed for service with the United States Mediterranean Squadron. Soon thereafter, the officers were assigned, the crew assembled, and stores for a lengthy cruise were loaded aboard. The ship was formally commissioned on 28 July 1855 under the command of Captain Charles H. Bell, a veteran naval officer. *Constellation* departed Hampton Roads, Virginia with orders to join the United States Mediterranean Squadron on 9 August 1855. Her complement included the full establishment prescribed by the Navy in 1854 of twenty officers, 235 sailors and forty-four marines.[12] One of the first entries in the Deck Log recorded that she had achieved a top speed of about twelve knots. After stopping briefly in the Azores, *Constellation* arrived off Gibraltar on 8 September 1855.[13]

For almost three years *Constellation* cruised the Mediterranean Sea to help protect American interests. Orderly Sergeant William P. Schwartz (alias Samuel P. Ramsey) of the Marine Guard explained the mission in a letter to his father. He wrote that in the event of trouble, "we will be obliged to take care of our Consul and other American citizens by displaying the Stars & Stripes . . . the appearance only of a man-of-war does wonders towards checking insults that would otherwise be offered to our people."[14] More often, however, the purpose for calling at port

Charles H. Bell, seen here as a Rear Admiral, was Captain of USS *Constellation* 1855–1858. (U.S. Naval Historical Center)

was purely diplomatic, and followed the established protocol of nations. The deck log entry for 7 December 1856 while in the Bay of Naples recorded, "At 9 saluted the Neapolitan Flag with 21 guns, which was returned by the Fort. Saluted the Neapolitan Admiral with 15 guns . . . The salute was returned by the Neapolitan Barque of War. The American Consul visited the ship."[15] Whatever its true purpose, the ship's arrival in port was sure to cause some notice, and no doubt aided American diplomatic missions.

Not all visitors came in an official capacity, however. Sergeant Schwartz wrote, "Our ship is in excellent condition, and is pronounced by all strangers to be the handsomest man-of-war they have ever seen." The captain, officers, and men of *Constellation* no doubt took pride in their vessel. Schwartz continued, "With the crew dressed very clean and neat, and the marines in full uniform make a very fine appearance, and attracts a great many visitors."[16]

Displaying what Captain Bell described in a letter to the Secretary of the Navy as "admirable sailing qualities," *Constellation* was often in company with the squadron flagship, USS *Congress*.[17] On 30 May 1856, the squadron's commander, Commodore Samuel L. Breese, wished to test the speed of the new sloop-of-war. Sergeant Schwartz reported the incident saying, "We convinced him [Breese] there was no use in trying to sail with us. We . . . ran round her [*Congress*] twice, and beat her so bad that the crew of the *Congress* were ashamed to come on board" after reaching port.[18]

Although the cruise was mostly uneventful, there was the occasional promise of action. After the commodore received "a report that American citizens required protection," during a revolution in Spain in July 1856, *Constellation* was dispatched to the port city of Malaga. Upon arrival, however, the men of *Constellation* "found everything tolerable quiet."[19] While patrolling in the Sea of Marmora the same year, *Constellation* rescued a barque in distress, for which the captain and crew received an official message in appreciation from the court of the Austrian emperor. *Constellation* was detached from the Mediterranean Squadron on 17 April 1858 and returned to the New York Navy Yard on 5 June.

Before the men whose terms of enlistment were nearing expiration could be discharged, *Constellation* took on supplies and was hurriedly sent to join the West Indies Squadron in the Caribbean Sea where a crisis was brewing. Her mission was to enforce the ban on the importation of African natives who were being smuggled to the United States from Cuba for the slave trade. She was also there to protect legitimate American merchant ships from being stopped and searched by the British Royal Navy. The British claimed they were only assisting the United States to enforce its own law, but it was perceived as a threat to American sovereignty and freedom of the seas. With the emergency alleviated by diplomatic negotiation and most of her crew serving on expired enlistments, the ship was finally sent home. The final entry in her deck log, dated 6 August 1858 in Boston, read:

> Hove up the anchor and stood up to the Navy Yard in tow of steam tugs. Ship in charge of pilot. Secured ship to the wharf . . . At 2:30 transferred to the receiving ship "Ohio" the Seamen, Ord. Sea., Landsmen and boys: Sent the Marines to the Marine Barracks and remainder of crew ashore on liberty.[20]

After leaving the ship, Captain Bell went on to other assignments. He eventually rose to the rank of Rear Admiral, and commanded the U.S. Pacific Squadron during the Civil War. *Constellation* was decommissioned on 13 August 1858, and underwent maintenance to correct the routine damages sustained during three years of patrol duty. Her next deployment would again find her cruising on a foreign station, but performing a remarkable mission that history books have often ignored.

USS *Constellation* at anchor in the Bay of Naples, circa 1856, by Tomaso de Simone.

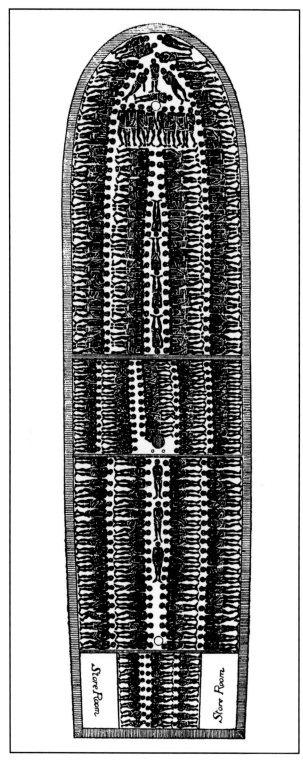

Stowage plan for a slave ship.

CHAPTER 3

SLAVE TRADE INTERDICTION PATROL

THE MAP OF AFRICA IN THE MID-NINETEENTH CENTURY WAS VASTLY different from that of today. Scores of tribes and petty kingdoms, which were often at war with one another, dotted the landscape. Hundreds of European, American, and Arab trading posts, called "factories," were found along the fringes of the continent. Many merchants were engaged in legitimate business trading for the products of the rain forest, such as palm oil, nuts, ivory, gums, and hardwoods to sell on the world market. Some traders, however, dealt in what they euphemistically called "black ivory." This export was shipped from isolated coves, usually at night and in great haste. Almost every tribe held prisoners, who were captured in battle or kidnapped from their rivals, as slaves. As a result, human labor was treated, and traded, like any other commodity. Many of these tribes conducted a lucrative business selling their captives in exchange for rum, textiles, jewelry, tobacco, iron hardware, firearms, and other goods. The trade was profitable: a healthy slave could be purchased in Africa for $50, and sold to the owners of plantations in Cuba, Brazil, or the southern United States at $200 or more.[1]

The African slave trade had flourished for centuries, and many Arab, English, Dutch, Spanish, Portuguese, and American merchants enjoyed its profits. By the 1800s, the world was awakening to the horror, death, and misery aboard slave ships. As the dispute over slavery as a system of labor edged the United States towards civil war, even many of the "peculiar institution's" supporters detested the inhumanity of the trade that supplied it.[2] In 1794, the United States was the first nation to take action against the international slave trade by prohibiting the outfitting of ships within its ports, if those vessels were destined to carry slaves from one foreign country to another.[3] In 1800 it became illegal for American citizens to carry African natives for sale from one country to another.[4] In 1807 Congress passed legislation to outlaw the trading of slaves between Africa and the United States, which became law in 1808.[5] In 1820 another Act of Congress declared that the transporting of slaves was piracy, and punishable by death.[6]

In 1807 Parliament also passed similar legislation for the British Empire. Great Britain became the leading advocate for suppressing the international slave trade, and other nations followed under British prodding. Spain, Portugal, and Brazil even allowed the Royal Navy to police their shipping and take the violators before mixed courts. France and the United States, however, refused to surrender their sovereignty, and directed their own naval squadrons to protect their legitimate merchantmen, as well as to capture slave traders.[7]

African natives who were sold into slavery were usually already weakened from the ordeal of their capture and being marched to a rendezvous where they were loaded on board ship. The ships in which they traveled "the middle passage" from Africa to the West Indies for forty to sixty days were truly Hell on Earth. Packed below deck in a dense mass, in a space generally only four feet high, the captives passed day and night in the most miserable conditions. They crouched in stifling heat, without ventilation or room enough to sleep, and used nearby tubs to heed the calls of nature. In such conditions, sickness spread rapidly. With daily allowances of food and water barely sufficient to keep them alive, any delay in crossing could result in the already meager rations being exhausted too soon. Starvation and sickness took their toll, and as many as one in five died. The bodies of those who perished were thrown overboard to the sharks before the ships reached port. The suffering was incredible.

With the governments of maritime nations passing and enforcing laws against the slave trade, it became a business too risky for individuals to undertake alone. Those engaged formed joint-stock companies. These companies employed men, and some women, from many occupations. Many worked for slaving enterprises as a sideline to the more respectable pursuits of their professions and may not have even been aware of what business they were assisting. Few actually dickered with African tribal leaders or haggled with plantation owners at either end of the process. Most worked in the "middle passage" as the captains, mates, seamen, cooks, doctors, and supercargoes on the vessels. There were also the merchants who shipped goods for trading with the native leaders, and the dealers in the rice, boilers, and medicines that were used on the ships for feeding and treating the slaves. There were stevedores who loaded the legitimate cargo aboard auxiliaries (explained below), and ship fitters that made alterations to the slaving vessels. There were shipping agents and brokers who processed the port documents, lawyers who defended those arrested, and even fictitious owners and captains who lent their names to voyages managed by others.

These companies also operated "auxiliaries" of various types. Hard to distinguish from ships engaged in legitimate business, these auxiliaries carried the goods used by the trading post agents to buy slaves and returned either empty, or with the stranded crews of captured and abandoned slave ships as passengers.

An ordinary merchant vessel had a galley and bunks, food and water, and medicines for perhaps a dozen men in the crew. Even when empty, slave smuggling ships were difficult to disguise. To sail the vessel and control the slaves, these ships had crews and accommodations for about twice the number needed on board a legitimate merchant ship. A slaver had to carry several thousand gallons of drinking water; tons of rice, farina, or ship's bread; and great quantities of preserved meat or fish. They also needed large boilers or furnaces, firewood or coal, and spoons, pails, and other items to cook and serve enough food to feed 700–900 captives for several weeks. Slave vessels also stored large quantities of medicines and disinfectants for treating diseases common to the natives and controlling epidemics that quickly spread among people confined in such crowded and unsanitary conditions. For keeping captives in line, slave vessels were equipped with a few swords and muskets, shackles to chain slaves to the deck, or iron grating over the hatches to keep them confined below.

The most damning evidence that even an empty ship was used in the slave trade was

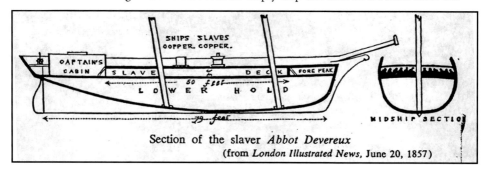

Section of the slaver *Abbot Devereux*
(from *London Illustrated News*, June 20, 1857)

Section of slaver showing slave deck.

the presence of a "slave deck." A ship built for legitimate commerce had most of its length occupied by the "hold," a large unbroken compartment usually measuring nine to ten feet from top to bottom, where cargo was stored. The main deck formed its top, with the captain's cabin aft, and the crew's quarters located forward in a forepeak. This arrangement would not do for a slaver, however. Slaves were not normally carried in the hold. There was no way to ventilate the bottom of the ship, and that is also where the food, water, and other supplies were stored. The solution was the installation of a middle deck dividing the hold into an upper and lower portion, with slaves above and provisions below. No ordinary merchantmen needed such a modification. After a slaver landed its agents at a trading post, it went back out to sea to wait while the captives were gathered. While waiting and avoiding the naval cruisers, the crew prepared the slave deck and other fittings. At the prearranged time and place, the ship would rendezvous with a flotilla of small boats loaded with captives rushing out from isolated coves, usually in the dark of night. After quickly loading, the slaver fled the area.[8]

After the U.S. government declared the importation of slaves illegal in 1808, and not wishing to surrender sovereignty to any other nation's armed forces, the U.S. Navy was ordered to enforce the law. Initially, the efforts centered on stopping the flow of slaves to American ports from the island of Cuba, a Spanish colony, which served as a transfer point for the shipments from Africa. *Constellation* had its first taste of this duty briefly, in 1858 in the Caribbean Sea. When the United States African Squadron was established in 1843, it expanded the Navy's interdiction area to the west coast of Africa.

The patrol of the African coast was considered a hardship duty, not only for the inhospitable climate, but also for the inhumanity of the slave trade that the officers and men saw at first hand. Captain Charles Bell commanded USS *Yorktown* on that station in 1845. In a letter to the Secretary of the Navy that year he wrote, "None but an eye-witness can form a conception of the horrors these poor creatures must endure in their transit across the ocean." He probably voiced the opinion of many naval officers when he continued, "I regret to say, that much of this misery is produced by our own countrymen."[9]

On 1 December *Yorktown* captured the brig *Pons* with 900 natives on board. One member of the prize crew, Master's Mate James C. Lawrence, USN, wrote, "Upon boarding this vessel, I felt such a load of misery fall upon my heart that I almost wished myself a wild beast, that I may escape the pain of sympathy that I felt for the sufferings of the wretched slaves."[10] Both Bell and Lawrence expressed further regret that, due to their weakened condition at the time of the ship's seizure, 150 of the liberated captives did not survive to be delivered to freedom at Monrovia. Certainly the experience moved them, and copies or excerpts of their letters found their way to abolitionist publications.

Secretary of the Navy Isaac Toucey designated *Constellation* flagship, or headquarters vessel, of the U.S. African Squadron on 20 April 1859.[11] When *Constellation* joined the squadron later that year the force included two more all-sail sloops-of-war, the 22-gun *Portsmouth* and 18-gun *Saratoga*. There were two steam-powered screw sloops, *San Jacinto* and *Mohican*, mounting 13 and 6 guns each, respectively. The two 6-gun steamers *Mystic* and *Sumter*, and the 2-gun supply ship *Relief* completed the list. Flag Officer William Inman was selected to command the squadron.[12] On 16 June Inman sent a message to Toucey from *Constellation* reading, "Sir, I have the honor to report that I have, this day, hoisted my Flag on board this Ship as directed by your Order."[13]

When Inman assumed command, he and his staff were quartered aboard *Constellation*, which was commanded by Captain John S. Nicholas. The ship's own complement consisted of some twenty other officers, as well as a crew of 243 enlisted sailors, and 44 men in the marine detachment.[14] Before departing Boston to join the squadron on 19 July,

Constellation's two 10-inch shell guns on pivot mounts on the spar deck were replaced by two 12-pounder howitzers. Eight of the iron water tanks were also removed and replaced with water stored in wooden casks. The reduction in armament and removal of the tanks required the loading of fifty tons of additional ballast.[15]

The U.S. African Squadron was part of a combined British and American effort to interdict the international slave trade. By agreement, only United States naval ships could stop and search vessels flying the American flag, but unflagged vessels were fair game for either nation's warships. American and British cruisers also cooperated by detaining suspicious vessels flying the other nation's colors until they could be boarded and searched by the proper authorities. As an incentive for performing this arduous duty, the U.S. government offered a bounty of $25.00 for every slave liberated, as well as prize money for each impounded vessel, to be divided among the crew according to rank. When a slave ship was seized, any African natives found on board were taken to Monrovia, Liberia and set free to colonize the region. The ship's crew was usually landed at the nearest port and released, while the captain and other officers were required to post a bond, or were returned immediately to the United States to wait for trial in U.S. District Court. The impounded vessels were taken to American ports where they were sold at auction by the government after adjudication by an Admiralty Court.

While the effectiveness of the overall operation may be debated, Inman proudly reported to the Secretary of the Navy on 14 August 1860, about midpoint in his twenty-two month tenure in command, the squadron rescued 1,600 slaves, nearly half the total freed between 1839 and 1859.[16] In fact, during 1860 alone, the squadron captured four fully loaded slavers. In all, Inman's squadron captured fourteen slave ships laden with 3,932 people on board. Even the flagship *Constellation* and her crew contributed to this effort with the capture of three ships, one of them loaded with 705 captives.[17]

Constellation took her first patrol station off the mouth of the Congo River on 21 November 1859, and it was not long before she had netted her first prize. One month later Inman reported to Secretary Toucey:

I have the honor to inform the Department that at 3 O'clock this morning, this ship captured a brig said to be the "Delicia," without colors or papers to show her nationality. She was completely fitted in all respects for the immediate embarcation [sic] of slaves . . .

According to the statement given by *Delicia*'s Chief Mate, the brig's captain landed at Little Black Point on 25 November to procure the cargo of slaves. The fifteen officers and crew remaining on board had just completed preparing the slave deck, and were heading for the coastal rendezvous when *Constellation* gave chase and upset the plan.[18]

Flag Officer William Inman, commander of the African Squadron 1859–1861. (U.S. Naval Historical Center)

Although many of the vessels *Constellation* and the rest of the African Squadron seized were empty, some were crammed with human cargo. On 26 September 1860, Inman reported "the capture of a Barque [*Cora*] with no flag and a cargo of 705 slaves."[19] While Inman's report lacks drama, the same can not be said of a description offered by Landsman William H. French. French was an enlisted member of the crew from 1859 to 1861. In a 16 September 1924 interview printed in the *Springfield Daily Republican* newspaper, French explained that as *Constellation* gave chase, *Cora* continued to flee despite the firing of blank cartridges and the splashing of 32-pound balls fired as warning shots, with clear orders for her to "heave to." French recalled that Inman, thinking the slaver would change course to escape in the darkness, employed some strategy of his own:

William H. French, pictured in 1926, served aboard *Constellation* 1859–1861.

> Commodore Inman called on the entire crew to trim the vessel for the chase . . . several of the crew manned the pumps to wet the sails so they would push the sloop along. Once in a while we'd fire a shot, but . . . we didn't try to hit them. The minute it became dark Commodore Inman ordered the course changed, and we nearly ran the Cora down. . . .

The excitement did not end after *Constellation* caught up with the slaver. *Cora* still had to be captured and her crew disarmed, and the mistreated victims had to be tended to, as they were in need of medical attention and food. Inman ordered Lieutenant Benjamin Loyall to lead a force of *Constellation*'s sailors and marines to take possession of the prize. French was a member of the boarding party, and continued his account saying,

> He [Lieutenant Loyall] sent us to pull up the hatches, and 705 natives came tumbling out of the hold, yelling and cringing. They ran forward and crouched on the bow . . . It was a fearful job, cleaning and doctoring those natives. They were nearly starved, but they responded to treatment and after keeping them awhile we landed them in Monrovia.[20]

The *Cora* was a 405-ton vessel built at Baltimore in 1851.[21] Registered in New York, she became a slaving vessel in 1860, only to be captured on 25 September of that same year. The following day the prize was placed under the command of Master Thomas H. Eastman, USN. He and his prize crew, consisting of Midshipman Walter B. Hall, four seamen, three ordinary seamen, four landsmen, and three marines from *Constellation* were ordered to land the captives at Monrovia, Liberia. Until they were turned over to the United States Agent there, *Constellation*'s men were ordered to "be careful for their maintenance, health and comfort, especially as to pure air," by Inman. Once landed, the African captives were to be freed.

Eastman and his crew were then to sail *Cora* to Norfolk, where the vessel was turned over to the Commandant of the Naval Station. John Latham, Morgan Fredericks, John Wilson, and Hans Olsen, *Cora*'s Captain, and First, Second and Third Mates, respectively, as well as four seamen of the crew, were turned over to the custody of the U.S. Marshals. The U.S. Attorney charged them with violating the acts of 1800 and 1820.[22]

Tried on 12 January 1861, the records of U.S. District Court, Southern New York district, show that Latham was still in custody in May, but subsequently escaped. Fredericks escaped before trial. Wilson and Olsen pleaded guilty to violating the act of 1800, and in November 1861 they were sentenced to ten months in prison and $500 fines each. The government did not prosecute the four sailors.[23]

Meanwhile, sectional conflict was dividing the nation. After Abraham Lincoln's election to the presidency in November 1860, Southern states began to secede. The nation was on the brink of civil war. On 21 May 1861, within weeks of the firing on Fort Sumter, *Constellation*'s crew encountered the last of the three slave ships they captured. As Flag Officer Inman was not then on board, Captain Nicholas sent the report informing Navy Secretary Gideon Welles of the incident saying, "I have the honor to report to you that I yesterday captured at Punta da Lenha the American brig *Triton*. She had no slaves on board, but every preparation for their reception had been made." *Triton*'s homeport was Charleston, South Carolina, one of the states in rebellion, and her seizure marked one of the Union Navy's first captures of the war.[24]

Shortly after *Triton*'s capture, Captain Nicholas was sent home because of failing health, and Captain Thomas A. Dornin assumed temporary command of the ship. With the Civil War now raging, the Navy needed every available vessel. *Constellation* was ordered home for repair and refit. When she arrived at the Portsmouth (New Hampshire) Navy Yard on 28 September 1861 Inman reported "all well," and requested permission from Secretary Welles to "strike his flag" and go home on leave.[25] Inman would retire without commanding again during the war. After relinquishing command of *Constellation* upon her return from Africa in 1861, Captain Dornin assumed command of the Baltimore Naval Station in April 1862 and was later promoted to Commodore.[26] A treaty was concluded with Great Britain in 1862 which allowed

Thomas A. Dornin, Captain of USS *Constellation* June–September 1861. (U.S. Naval Historical Center)

the Royal Navy to board and search American ships suspected of smuggling slaves.

Constellation's crew was not immune to the divided loyalties being experienced by many Americans. In October 1861, the Navy asked all of the ship's officers to affirm their allegiance to the United States. Although most continued to serve the Union, Lieutenant Loyall and Midshipman Walter R. Butt declined, and like one fifth of the officers in the Navy, either resigned or were dismissed from the service. Loyall and Butt went on to serve with distinction in the Confederate Navy.[27] The war caused the two Marine Corps officers on board at the time of the Cora capture to choose different sides. While Captain Isaac Doughty served the Union and was later promoted to Major, First Lieutenant John R. F. Tattnall offered his services to the South. His appointment in the Confederate forces, however, was approved before he tendered his resignation from the U.S. Marine Corps. While serving aboard USS San Jacinto, he learned of his appointment and attempted to resign. His request was declined and he was instead placed in confinement as a prisoner of war. Tattnall had to wait until exchanged on 13 February 1862 before accepting his commission and assuming his duties as an officer of Confederate marines.[28]

While both Tattnall and his father, Commodore Josiah Tattnall, went South, the war divided the Nicholas family. Although some in the crew shared a rumor that Captain Nicholas, a Virginian by birth, was actually replaced after the start of hostilities due to his suspected Southern sympathies, he remained loyal and served in the Union Navy throughout the war. His son, Wilson Nicholas, however, served as a Captain with the First Maryland Infantry Regiment, and later on the staff of Brigadier General Bradley T. Johnson, in the Confederate Army. Ironically, the younger Nicholas was a native Northerner, having been born at the New York Navy Yard in Brooklyn.[29]

When Constellation put to sea again, it would be to help preserve the Union. Her officers and men would be on alert to engage enemy vessels they knew could be manned by former shipmates. In the end, the war would also decide the fate of the labor system that was fed by the trade Constellation had fought so hard against for more than two years.

Marine Captain Isaac Doughty (above) and Lieutenant John R. F. Tattnall were both serving on board Constellation when the Cora was captured. During the Civil War, Doughty fought for the Union and Tattnall for the Confederacy.

Commander Henry K. Thatcher commanded *Constellation* March 1862-July 1863, and was promoted to Commodore in July 1862. (U.S. Naval Historical Center)

CHAPTER 4

CIVIL WAR SERVICE

USS *CONSTELLATION* RETURNED TO BALTIMORE'S INNER HARBOR on 2 July 1999 restored to her proper sloop-of-war configuration. She is not only the last all-sail powered warship built by the U.S. Navy, but is also the only surviving Civil War-era naval vessel still afloat. Like many ships of the Union Navy, she fought in none of the war's naval engagements. Her crew, like those serving on the hundreds of other ships in the fleet, fought only boredom, and drilled constantly to be ready in the event they would ever see combat. Many ask, what was *Constellation's* role in the War Between the States; did she ever fire a gun in anger; and, how did she help win the war and restore the Union?

On 12 April 1861, as Confederate forces prepared to fire on Fort Sumter, USS *Constellation* was the flagship of a naval squadron of eight vessels on foreign station. As such, she made one of the Union Navy's first captures when her crew seized the slave smuggling brig *Triton* off the coast of Africa. At the beginning of the war, *Constellation* was one of only 90 vessels on the Navy list. Between the firing on Fort Sumter in April and the end of 1861, the navy grew to 264 ships. By 1865, *Constellation* was one of 670 vessels in the Union fleet.[1] The need for ships was necessitated by the missions assigned to the Navy: blockading 3,500 miles of Confederate coastline and seizing Southern harbors; gaining control of the western rivers; and cruising foreign waters protecting merchant shipping and other U.S. overseas interests. In the course of the war, *Constellation* performed two of these three missions.

Because her deep draft and lack of steam power limited her use in coastal waters, *Constellation* was not slated for blockade duty at the war's start. After being placed back in commission on 26 February 1862, she prepared for deployment to the Mediterranean Sea with 20 officers, 255 sailors, and 45 marines. Before November 1863, however, the enlistments of new recruits and a band raised the number of sailors to 283![2] She had orders to serve as a deterrent to Confederate commerce raiders, to show the flag in European waters and to protect American interests. As the last all-sail ship to be built for the U.S. Navy, it was hoped that her endurance and cruising ability could be used to advantage on the open sea where she would not be tied to coaling stations, and perhaps outperform some less efficient steam ships. Yeoman Moses A. Safford would later reflect the thoughts of the crew about *Constellation's* lack of engines and armor by writing in his diary, "Before this war is over I may see as much fighting as any of them. Within a week we may go down at our guns like the men in the *Cumberland* in a fight with a modern ship."[3]

Commander Henry K. Thatcher was designated to command *Constellation* in late 1861, and a short time thereafter, he began assembling his staff and supervising preparation of the ship for sea. On 11 March 1862, *Constellation* departed Portsmouth on her new assignment. Mounting 22 guns, her main battery still consisted of the sixteen 8-inch shell guns and four 32-pounders she carried since being commissioned in 1855. While undergoing repair and refit during the winter of 1861–1862, the 12-pounders that had been positioned on the spar deck during the African Squadron cruise were replaced. Thatcher had pleaded with the Ordnance Bureau to provide him with weapons that would allow *Constellation* to engage enemy steam-powered vessels escaping into the wind, and therefore out of the range of her 8-inch broadside guns. The request resulted in the mounting of two rifled guns on the spar deck on pivot carriages. One 30-pounder Parrott rifle was mounted on the forecastle, while one 20-pounder Parrott was placed at the stern.[4] For arming the ship's boats, *Constellation* also took on two more 12-pounder Dahlgren bronze boat howitzers, for a total of three.[5]

One of the Confederate commerce raiders then preying upon Union merchant ships early in the war was CSS *Sumter*, which was under the command of Commander Raphael Semmes, CSN. Pursued by Union warships and in need of repair, the rebel sought safe haven at Gibraltar instead of nearby Algeciras, Spain. As Yeoman Safford explained, "The Spanish regard the *Sumpter* [sic] as a pirate, and would seize her as such in their own ports, but the British are more partial in their attitude toward her."[6] Immediately upon arriving on 19 April 1862, *Constellation* joined U.S. warships *Kearsarge*, *Tuscarora*, and *Ino* in isolating the Confederate cruiser in port. *Kearsarge* actually went into Gibraltar harbor and moored directly astern of *Sumter* for a time. No shots were fired in the neutral port, but Midshipman Charles F. Blake of *Constellation* reported an encounter in which, "The *Sumpter's* [sic] officers one evening struck up 'Dixie,' and then the *Kearsarge's* commenced the 'Star Spangled Banner'." The exchange escalated. The captain of *Kearsarge* was returning to his ship after a visit on shore, "When the crew of one of *Sumter's* boats commenced cursing him as only such scoundrels can do."[7]

Knowing that to venture out of the harbor was to invite destruction, by 23 April Commander Thatcher was able to report to Secretary of the Navy Gideon Welles, "The *Sumter* has been laid up at Gibraltar and abandoned by her captain and officers, except for a small party left in charge of her, the crew having been discharged."[8] With *Sumter* a reduced threat, *Constellation* began patrolling the Mediterranean Sea. Henry Thatcher was promoted to the grade of Commodore after the Navy reestablished that rank in the summer of 1862, and he remained in command of *Constellation* for another year. In addition to protecting Union merchant ships from Confederate cruisers, *Constellation* participated in the attempt to prevent the rebel navy from taking possession of ships purchased from European shipbuilders. One of these was the British-built *Southerner*. Commodore Thatcher recounted this endeavor in a message to Navy Secretary Welles that read:

> I have learned . . . that a very fast steamer, said to be called the *Southerner*, has been built in England, destined for a Confederate cruiser against United States commerce in the Mediterranean, and . . . a rebel commander, T. Jefferson Page, late of the U.S. Navy, is now at Florence . . . awaiting the steamer with the intention of assuming command.[9]

Although she saw no combat in engagements with the Confederate Navy, this report of 29 June 1863 indicates how many of the Union's "unsung hero" ships contributed to the Northern victory at sea.

Captain Henry S. Stellwagen replaced Commodore Thatcher as *Constellation's* commander on 18 July 1863.[10] Thatcher went on to command the 48-gun steam and sail frigate USS *Colorado*, and to lead a division in Admiral Porter's attack on Fort Fisher in January 1865. Thatcher was promoted to Rear Admiral before the end of the war. *Constellation* remained on the Mediterranean station until the Navy Department sent Captain Stellwagen orders in May 1864 to report with his ship to the commander of the

Captain Henry Stellwagen (seen here in the rank of Commander) commanded USS *Constellation* July 1863-January 1865. (U.S. Naval Historical Center)

West Gulf Blockading Squadron.[11] En route, she assumed missions keeping within her capabilities. As Yeoman Safford described:

> We were to cruise about the West Indies trying to capture Rebel privateers and cruisers and blockade-runners. The process of reasoning . . . seems to be that our ship is supposed to be in European waters, and there is no United States warship resembling her cruising about here, and consequently she might approach closely to a Rebel vessel or blockade runner without exciting suspicion . . . It is conceived that we might surprise such vessels and capture or sink them.[12]

Although they engaged no enemy vessels, they did encounter the *Mersey* of Liverpool, England. The brig had been dismasted in a storm and was in distress. *Constellation*'s men furnished navigation instruments, provisions, and medical assistance to the crew of the stricken vessel. Captain Gensen credited the assistance with saving his ship and crew from immediate peril, thus enabling him to reach the nearest port safely. Although he thought the incident not worth mentioning to the Navy Department, an official letter of thanks was sent to Captain Stellwagen by R. B. Lamb, Her Britannic Majesty's Consul in St. Thomas, on 10 November 1864.[13]

As soon as she arrived at Mobile Bay on 27 November 1864, *Constellation* was ordered to the naval yard at Pensacola, Florida. Two days later, after giving the ship a good scraping and scrubbing, the crew was called to quarters and stood inspection by Rear Admiral David G. Farragut. With the terms of service of most of her sailors nearing expiration, and the ship not suited for blockade service in coastal waters, Farragut ordered *Constellation* to the Union naval base at Norfolk, Virginia. After taking on water and supplies, she headed north for decommissioning. Despite the fate that awaited the ship, the journey did not prove uneventful.

When *Constellation* sailed into Havana harbor in mid December, both officers and men had no difficulty in identifying those "suspicious steamers reputed to be blockade runners." One of the vessels they observed in Havana had a very familiar appearance to the veterans among the crew. Captain Stellwagen believed her to be the former *Harriet Lane*, a U.S. Revenue Cutter that had been transferred to the Navy early in the war. *Harriet Lane* was subsequently captured by the Confederates off Galveston, Texas and converted to blockade running. In December 1864, Stellwagen reported to Secretary Welles that the former Revenue Cutter was now "under the English flag and called the *Lavinia*." In a neutral port, however, the Union Navy was powerless to recapture her.[14]

Constellation arrived at Hampton Roads on Christmas Day. Two days later Captain Stellwagen filed a report that arguably recounted the most exciting event of the war experienced by his crew. On 19 December the men went to "general quarters" while the ship was positioned at 32° Latitude, 38° Longitude at sea:

I discovered coming out of a dense fog what appeared to be a Blockade Runner, standing to the windward . . . I immediately made all sail and gave chase. As soon as prudent I fired one blank cartridge. She continued her course and in a few moments commenced firing at her. Fired seven shots from the Forward pivot Parrott Rifle and two from the Forward thirty-two, all of which fell short but in good range.[15]

Yeoman Safford's diary recorded the same engagement from an enlisted man's perspective. With his customary flair, he wrote:

A typical blockade runner - painted white and very sharply built . . . waiting with fires banked for assurance from the shore that the coast was clear to run in. When, however, our ship headed in her direction, smoke began to come out of her funnel and she made off to windward at good speed . . . we kept after her with all our sail and fired a gun for her to heave to. She did not accept the invitation or heed the warning.[16]

As the members of the crew already knew, this incident only underscored the fact that the lack of steam-power only limited *Constellation*'s continued value to the Navy. In a correspondence dated Christmas Day of 1864, when the ship arrived off Fortress Monroe, Stellwagen recommended to Secretary Welles that *Constellation* be converted to a supply vessel.[17] While it was clear the Navy intended to remove her from the cruiser force, there were other uses in store for this all sail-powered ship.

Soon after *Constellation*'s arrival in Hampton Roads, the crew began preparations to place the vessel in the navy yard for repairs. On 27 January 1865, Stellwagen reported that the men whose enlistments had expired were "paid off" and discharged; the remainder of the crew was transferred to the sail frigate USS *St. Lawrence*, while the officers were sent on leave to await orders.[17] Captain Stellwagen took his leave at home in Philadelphia. He did not have long to wait. Within two weeks, he sent a letter to the Navy Department acknowledging his receipt of orders to report to Boston. From there he would take command of the screw sloop USS *Pawnee* and report to Rear Admiral John A. Dahlgren of the South Atlantic Blockading Squadron.[18]

Constellation finished the war as a Receiving Ship at Norfolk. Receiving ships were obsolete vessels the Navy stationed at yards and port cities to act as floating barracks. New recruits were assigned to them to receive their initial issue of uniforms and individual equipment, and undergo some rudimentary naval training while waiting to join the crew of an active unit of the fleet. Sailors nearing the expiration of their terms of enlistment were also housed there to wait for their discharges and final pay. Ordinary Seaman David Cady, ship's number 356, was a typical example of the hundreds of veterans who spent their last days of naval service on board. His discharge certificate from the Receiving Ship *Constellation* dated 2 May 1865 also reflects he was provided passage to Baltimore following his release. *Constellation* functioned in this capacity at Norfolk and Philadelphia until 1869.

She may not have been in any storied naval engagements, but on the ledger of Civil War achievements, *Constellation* made one of the Union Navy's first captures, protected Union merchantmen from rebel commerce raiders, and helped to enforce the blockade of the Confederacy. Having fired her guns in anger only once, her days as a fighting ship were at an end.

Ordinary Seaman David
Cady.

Discharge of O. S. Cady from
the Receiving Ship
Constellation, 2 May 1865.

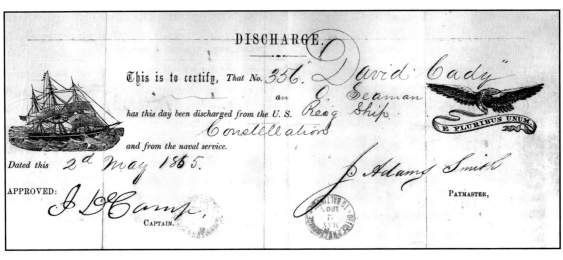

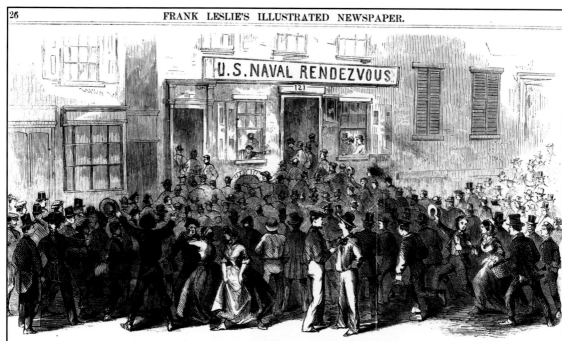

RECRUITING FOR THE NAVY IN NEW YORK—SCENE OUTSIDE THE RECRUITING RENDEZVOUS IN CHERRY STREET.—SEE PAGE 22.

LUCILLE DE VERNET:

A TALE OF

WOMAN'S HATE.

CHAPTER XVI.

a small but commodious room, the furniture of which was more nducive to comfort than show, and where, though early autumn, right fire burnt in the polished stove, which reflected manifold its glittering surface the high meandering flames, now mounting

whisper, hope. I will to the valley. I will go, if only to pardon her."

The valet entered with the letters; d'Almaine caught them eagerly, his quick eye glanced over the superscriptions, then throwing them unopened on the table, again sank listlessly on the sofa.

The countess entered in becoming deshabille; she drew near the conch, and touching his forehead with her lips, saying blandly, "Good morning, my son; I am happy to see the black ribbon discarded from the wounded arm, although it did give an interesting feature to your appearance."

An unintelligible response fell from the count's lips as he placed himself at the breakfast table. He was pale and haggard, and apparently without appetite, for he helped himself to game, which, after mincing in his plate, he sent away nearly untouched; a peach

A dozen words from her would convince me. Tell me why is she banished from her home?"

"I have told you," said the countess, haughtily. "Because she disobeyed my will in reference to the Duke de Paleron, and she returns not here, nor to any dwelling of mine until she consents to become his wife."

"The Duke de Paleron!" hissed through the closed teeth of the count. "Madame," he added, turning sternly towards her, "as your heart, if it still exists, why you should desire such a union. You admit he is the destroyer of your son's happiness, would you sacrifice your daughter's to him also?"

An angry and vindictive answer had risen to the countess's lips, but its utterance was stopped by the entrance of Vigna, to announce the arrival of the dresses from Madame Boloin.

Prospective recruits crowd a Naval Rendezvous in 1861. (U.S. Naval Historical Center)

CHAPTER 5

UNCLE SAM'S WEB FEET

THE U.S. NAVY EXPANDED IN STRENGTH FROM 89 TO 264 VESSELS IN 1861, and ultimately to some 670 by 1865. To man this fleet, the Navy grew in strength from about 9,000 to 22,000 officers and men in 1861, and by the end of the war, more than 118,000 men had been in Union naval service. To meet the need for manpower, the U.S. Navy accepted men of all colors and backgrounds, and this diversity was reflected in the crew of *Constellation* during the Civil War. Most of the ship's recruits came from harbor towns, primarily in New England. They included both native and foreign-born individuals and represented a variety of social backgrounds and skills. A recruit had to stand at least four feet, eight inches in height, and pass a brief physical examination before signing his "shipping article," or enlistment papers. Young men under the age of eighteen who wished to join the Navy had to have consent of parents or guardian, and the average Civil War sailor was twenty-five years of age. The usual term of enlistment was three years or one cruise, and a sailor could expect to be at sea most of that time. The naval enlisted man was known as a "Jack Tar," a nickname of British origin adopted in America for the common sailor in naval service.[1]

"Landsman" was the rank of naval recruits. They endured with constant harassment from their more seasoned comrades and performed the dirtiest and most menial tasks. Landsmen scraped and scrubbed the decks, worked the pumps, cleaned the manger, and polished the guns. Landsmen also did the heavy work, like weighing and stowing the anchors, hauling on the lines that "braced" the yards and adjusted the sails, and manning the gun tackles. *Constellation*'s Civil War crew included sixty-nine sailors in the rank of Landsman. After at least three years' experience a Landsman, or Boy if at least age fifteen, could be promoted to Ordinary Seaman. The duties of an O. S. included those that required more skill and knowledge, like handling and splicing lines, and working aloft on the masts and yards. There were eighty-two Ordinary Seamen listed in the crew of *Constellation* in March of 1863. Promotion to Seaman meant the sailor had at least six years' experience and had demonstrated that he "knew the ropes." When fully rigged, the average ship of *Constellation*'s size had at least four miles of rope, and the Seaman knew them all by name and use, as well as every shipboard task instinctively. The ship's Civil War Muster Roll lists the names of fifty-seven Seamen.[2]

The most reliable and experienced sailors were appointed Petty Officers, and occupied positions of intermediate authority. Leading Petty Officers, such as the Master-at-Arms, Yeoman, the various Mates (except for Master's Mates, who held warrant officer appointments) and Stewards of the staff officers, were like sergeants in the Army or Marine Corps, both in authority and responsibility. There was a lower level of petty officer that paralleled the rank of Corporal in the Army and Marines. These were the Quarter Masters, Quarter Gunners, Captains of the Forecastle, Tops, Afterguard and Hold, Coxswains, Armorers, Coopers, Painters, and Master-at-Arms' Corporals. Unlike in the Army, the Navy had a rat-

**Two hundred eighty-three "Jack Tars" like these served
in *Constellation*'s Civil War crew. (Library of Congress)**

ing for Cooks, who also held petty officer ranks. The line petty officers "ran" the ship, and were relied on for their advice on safety and maintenance by the captain and officers. Other petty officers were appointed based on their previously acquired skills or training to perform special duties or staff assignments in the various ship's departments. In all, the Muster Roll lists a total of fifty-nine petty officers appointed among the *Constellation*'s crew by March 1863.[3]

The Master-at-Arms was the naval counterpart of a regimental Sergeant Major in the Army, being primarily responsible for discipline among the crew. John Glenn of Troy, New York, Ship's Number 255, was appointed *Constellation*'s Master-at-Arms in November 1861, and served throughout the Civil War cruise. He was said to have once been a boxer. He was described by his messmate Yeoman Safford as a "very jolly, good natured man although he has a reputation of having been 'on his muscle,'" due to his tendency to resort to brute strength.[4]

Moses A. Safford of Kittery, Maine was a practicing lawyer when the war began. He had hoped to secure the rank of Acting Master, one of the few naval officer grades available to volunteers, based on his education, and previous experience on merchant ships and in the militia. Instead, he accepted the appointment as ship's Yeoman on 26 December 1861, and was assigned Ship's Number 264. Unlike in the modern Navy where a Yeoman performs administrative and clerical duties, in the old Navy he had charge of the material and equipment necessary for the maintenance and operation of the vessel, and was the ranking staff petty officer. Working under direct supervision of the Executive Officer, the Yeoman saw to the acquisition, inventory, and issue of supplies; maintained accountability for the stores used by the various departments of the ship; and was a trained sailor. Safford kept a detailed diary of his experience aboard *Constellation* from 11 March 1862 to 27 January 1865. His diary gives the petty officers' perspective of life aboard a man-of-war during the Civil War.[5]

Young men between the ages of thirteen and eighteen could join the Navy as Boys or Apprentices. Although they required parental consent, some were as young as eleven, and every port had many orphans and runaways eager to volunteer. An old Navy adage said, "It took six years to make a seaman." At that rate, a typical recruit would be well into his mid-twenties before attaining the necessary proficiency level. The Apprentice rank was a means for the Navy to develop fully trained sailors at a younger age. By regulation, boys could make up no more than 5 percent of a ship's crew, and *Constellation*'s Muster Roll for March 1862 lists seventeen Boys. Fifteen year-old Arthur Phelps, Ship's Number 229, from Old Cambridge, Massachusetts was a typical Apprentice. Enlisting on 5 November 1861 in Boston as a 2nd Class Boy, he reported on board *Constellation* from the Receiving Ship *Ohio* in March 1862.

Boys learned seamanship on the job. They also acted as messengers, cook's helpers, sick bay attendants, and officers' servants. In combat, or during drill, the ship's boys carried powder cartridges from the passing scuttles to the guns. Because anything small in size was referred to as a "monkey," this hazardous activity earned them the nickname Powder Monkeys. At 7:30 every morning, the boys assembled for inspection by the master-at-arms. They were expected to have clean faces and hands, hair combed, and uniforms clean and tidy. Following inspection, the boys climbed to the top of the masthead, and back down the other side. This exercise was done to keep them agile for their duties. The Powder Monkey's duty required someone who was fast, and able to quickly get in and out of tight areas: a job perfectly suited for teenaged boys. They also had to be brave, and at least two of the Navy's Boys were awarded the Medal of Honor for heroism during the Civil War. They were boys who did a man-sized job.[6]

Boys were not the only potential recruits who were restricted in number. The Navy, unlike the Army, accepted blacks as regular members before the Emancipation Proclamation. Furthermore, unlike the soldiers, black sailors had always received the same pay as their white shipmates. Before the Civil War, the U.S. Navy tried to restrict the number of black men to 5 percent of any ship's crew. At the war's start, the African Americans who enlisted were mostly free men living in northern port cities. The need for manpower led Navy Secretary Gideon Welles to suggest to the North Atlantic Blockading Squadron commander that he open stations ashore for recruiting "contrabands," as blacks who fled slavery for the protection of Union forces were called. By the end of the war, African Americans accounted for more than 10 percent of the Navy's lower rank strength. *Constellation*'s Muster Rolls show as many as fifteen blacks served on board during the Civil War.

Among the most experienced African American sailors aboard *Constellation* in the Civil War was James Evans, Ship's Number 40. Evans enlisted in Boston on 15 November

Seventeen "Powder Monkeys" served on *Constellation* in the Civil War. (U.S. Naval Historical Center)

Fifteen of *Constellation*'s sailors in the Civil War were African American. (U.S. Army Military History Institute)

1861 as a Seaman, indicating he had previous naval experience. By March 1863, he had been promoted to petty officer with the rating of Coxswain, one of seven authorized for a ship of *Constellation*'s size. Like most blacks in the crew, he was most likely a free man before the war began.[7]

In addition to the sailors, all large ships and naval bases also had marine detachments. During the Civil War the Marine Corps grew from 1,800 to about 4,100 officers and men. *Constellation*'s Muster Roll showed forty-five members in the Marine Guard from 1862 to 1865, commanded by Second Lieutenant Robert O'Neil Ford. In descending order of rank, there was one Lieutenant, one Orderly Sergeant, one Sergeant, three Corporals, thirty-six Privates, and three Musicians. Sergeant Timothy Whelan, who enlisted at the Boston Marine Barracks on 3 June 1861 for a four-year term (under the alias of Wayland) was assigned to the Marine Guard with roster number 3. He also kept a diary of his tour of duty in the Civil War on board *Constellation*.[8]

The marines were drilled in manning all the guns. Orderly Sergeant Schwartz wrote that he "spent much of the time exercising the large guns and preparing everything for action in case of need." When the ship's company was called to quarters, some marines could be distributed among the gun divisions, or could comprise an entire gun crew. Schwartz was quick to point out that he "was particularly busy . . . in making the marines perfect at large as well as small arms." The marines were usually formed into a single division under their lieutenant on the spar deck. From there, the captain could order them into the rigging as sharpshooters, to support boarding parties or repel enemy boarders on the spar deck, or conduct operations ashore.[9]

Although they participated in few major land battles, marines from the blockading squadrons conducted numerous raids along the Confederate coast throughout the Civil War. To improve their readiness, *Constellation*'s marines practiced launching these operations regularly while cruising the Mediterranean. Yeoman Safford recorded one such exercise in 1862 saying, "All our boats are put over and completely armed and equipped, and are landed through the surf. Everyone gets wet, but the imitation of landing an armed expedition was really very credibly done."[10]

When not training or engaged in battle, marines provided the officers with a force capable of stopping fights that resulted from the personality clashes that surely arose among large numbers of men confined in a small area. As Sergeant Schwartz explained in another letter, the marines were charged with "keeping order in the ship." They also guarded the Captain's Cabin, the Spirit Room, and the Brig. These police duties often raised the ire of their sailor-shipmates and fueled inter-service rivalry.[11]

Constellation's complement of officers, aside from the Captain, usually numbered about twenty. The social stratification of the U.S. Navy's officer corps is reflected by the assignment of their quarters on the berth deck. First came the Line officers, who were responsible for sailing and fighting the ship, and commanding the various divisions of the crew when at quarters. They were housed in the five staterooms on the starboard, or right hand, side of the Wardroom, as one looks forward. The senior, or First Lieutenant, was the second in command until the Navy created the rank of Lieutenant Commander in July 1862; it then became the rank for *Constellation*'s Executive Officer. He occupied the largest and forward-most

Second (later First) Lieutenant Robert O'Neil Ford commanded *Constellation*'s Marines during the Civil War.

The forty-four enlisted men of *Constellation*'s Marine Guard wore dress uniforms similar to these marines in 1864. (Library of Congress)

Lieutenant Edwin H. Miller, one of *Constellation's* **line officers in the Civil War.**

stateroom, followed aft by the four lieutenants according to seniority. The Civil or Staff officers were in charge of the ship's specialized departments and occupied the staterooms of the port side of the wardroom. The Surgeon managed the medical department. The Paymaster, formerly called the Purser, accounted for the crew's payroll, purchased supplies and equipment, and sold comfort items and sundries to the crew while at sea. The Master, formerly called the Sailing Master, was responsible for navigation and was usually a transitional rank for line officers between Passed Midshipman and Lieutenant. The Captain's Secretary was the ship's administrative officer. A Marine Corps First or Second Lieutenant was assigned to command the Marine Guard.[12]

Until the Navy assimilated line and staff into a unified rank structure, the relationships between the two could get confusing. Staff officers held ranks comparable to line officers, but without command responsibility. For instance, a Surgeon or Paymaster with at least twelve years experience was equivalent in pay and grade to a Commander, while one with less than twelve years was comparable to a Lieutenant. A "Passed Assistant" Surgeon or Paymaster was equivalent to a Master, as was a Captain's Secretary. The rank of Master was just below Lieutenant, and eventually became Lieutenant Junior Grade in later years. The Assistant Surgeon and Paymaster were equivalent in grade to a Passed Midshipman. To meet the needs of an expanded officer corps, the Secretary of the Navy could commission Volunteer Lieutenants and Acting Masters to hold appointments, like their Army counterparts, that lasted only for the duration of the war, and ranked below regular lieutenants and masters respectively.[13]

The Navy's 1854 *Tables of Allowances* for *Constellation's* officers included four junior officers in the ranks of Passed Midshipmen, Midshipmen, and Master's Mates, whose quarters were located just outside the wardroom. Midshipmen were the men who had completed their academic course work at the Naval Academy, and functioned as junior line officers while waiting to take their final examinations for

Acting Master Eugene B. Mallett served on *Constellation* **from 1861 to 1865.**

Henry C. Cochrane commanded the ship's Marine Guard 1867–1868 as a First Lieutenant.

graduation. If they attained qualifying scores on those tests, they became Passed Midshipmen until promoted to Master or Lieutenant. In 1862 the Navy created the rank of Ensign to replace the grade of Passed Midshipman.

Midshipman Charles F. Blake was assigned to *Constellation* from 5 March 1862 to 14 June 1863, while awaiting examination. After being ordered home for and passing the test, he was reassigned to USS *Wabash*, where he was promoted to Ensign. He was later wounded at the battle of Mobile Bay while serving on USS *Brooklyn*. Blake also kept a journal of his time on *Constellation*, giving us a junior officer's glimpse of duty during the Civil War.[14]

Master's Mates, Paymaster's, and Captain's Clerks were considered Warrant Officers, who assisted the Master, Paymaster, and Captain's Secretary, respectively, and were the staff officer equivalents in grade to the Midshipmen. The last four Warrant Officers, who occupied quarters in Steerage, represented the lowest rung on the officer ladder. The Boatswain and Gunner on the line side, and the Carpenter and Sail Maker on the staff side, were the technical experts of long experience in the ranks responsible for sailing, fighting, and maintaining the ship and its equipment. To ease the shortage of officers and midshipmen created by wartime expansion, ships' captains were authorized to appoint deserving petty officers to Acting warrant officer billets. They were given duties, pay and afforded the respect of officers, but unless the Department of the Navy made their appointments permanent, these individuals reverted to their enlisted ranks at the end of the cruise.[15]

At the head of the ship's chain of command was the Captain. The Captain's Cabin aft on the gun deck housed the commanding officer's living and working quarters, and reflected his status. On the port side were his office, pantry, and washroom. The large room in the center served as both a dining room and parlor, and a place in which he could confer with his officers, conduct other official business, or entertain guests and visiting dignitaries. On the starboard side were his stateroom and water closet. The desk and work area for Captain's Secretary or Clerk was also located in the cabin. The configuration of the cabin could be modified to comfortably house both the captain and flag officer when *Constellation* served as a flagship of a squadron.

The Captain was responsible for the training, safety, and discipline of the crew. Because he was also responsible for their health and welfare, no one else exerted more influence on the men's morale than the commanding officer. Because his cabin was authorized to have a rug or painted canvas covering on the deck, getting summoned to see the captain was sometimes referred to as being "called on the carpet." Ships and their crews often reflected the personalities of their captains, and *Constellation* was no exception. As Yeoman Safford recorded in 1863, "This forenoon Captain Stellwagen called all hands to muster and read his order from Secretary Welles to assume command of the ship. He said that Commodore Thatcher gave the ship a good name."[16]

As the only surviving naval vessel of the American Civil War, USS *Constellation* recalls the often-overlooked contributions of the United States Navy and Marine Corps in that conflict. President Abraham Lincoln once said in a speech, "Nor must Uncle Sam's web feet be forgotten. At all the watery margins they have been present. Wherever the ground has been a little damp they have made their tracks." Today, their tracks remain indelibly printed on the decks of *Constellation*.

Paymaster's Clerk William E. Cox in 1865.

Acting Boatswain John R. Hunter.

Constellation's sailors and marines would have resembled
those on board this ship. (U.S. Naval Historical Center)

CHAPTER 6

LIFE AT SEA

W HAT WAS LIFE LIKE FOR UNCLE SAM'S WEB FEET? UPON ENLIST-
ing, each sailor received his issue of uniforms in a canvas sea bag; a hammock, hair mattress
and two blankets; and a metal cup, one-quart bucket, knife, fork, and spoon. He was then
sent to a "Receiving Ship" to wait for his assignment to an active warship while undergoing
some introductory training. When a sailor was transferred to his new ship of assignment,
he signed the muster book and was assigned his personal "ship's number." That number
corresponded to his various duty assignments listed on the station, quarter, and fire bills,
both at sea and in port. He was also assigned to a watch, or shift, that determined when
he was to work, eat, sleep, and go on liberty ashore. After the administrative procedures
were satisfied, the sailor was given his berthing assignment. The hammock used by Union
sailors was 72 inches long and 30 inches wide. Suspended from the overhead by a rope
that passed through twelve grommets on each end, it was ideally suited to minimize the
roll effect of the vessel on those trying to sleep. The administrative and training require-
ments for the marines were taken care of at the nearest marine barracks before they were
assigned to a ship.[1]

The berth deck served for sleeping, eating, and recreation for the watch not on duty.
The enlisted members of the crew were quartered between the sickbay, forward, and the
wardroom, or officers' quarters, aft. In order to accommodate everyone, the sailors' daily
life was planned around the watch schedule. Yeoman Safford described the arrangement in
his diary by saying, "Who would believe after observing the bustle and turmoil of the day
that 300 men could be so quiet at night with half of them 'on watch.'"[2] On a wooden
man-of-war this deck was subject to constant dampness. When combined with high summer temperatures and the body heat of 300 men, conditions could get somewhat uncom-
fortable. Safford remarked, "At night the Berth Deck is like a baker's oven." Portholes
allowed some ventilation when at anchor in a harbor, but were closed while at sea. In summer, a canvas "wind sail" was installed above the hatch to catch the breeze and funnel it
below to increase ventilation. Otherwise, members of the crew tried to remain on the spar
deck or gun deck as long as possible before retiring.[3]

The typical workday aboard a Civil War-era warship like the *Constellation* usually
began at 5:00 a.m. when the marine musician sounded "Reveille." The ship's master-at-
arms, or one of his corporals, and the boatswain's mate of the current watch on duty then
ran around the berth deck shouting and slapping hammocks to wake the sleeping sailors.
The men got up and lashed their hammocks and bedding into a tight bundle and carried
them to the spar deck. There, they were stored along the bulwarks behind the rails. This
arrangement provided some additional protection from small arms fire and flying splinters
from enemy cannon fire in battle. A well-trained crew was able to rise, lash their hammocks, and place them in the hammock rails in seven minutes.[4]

After the hammocks were secured, the crew got out sand, brooms, holystones, and buckets to wash down the decks. The berth deck was usually scrubbed with salt water. Teams under the direction of a boatswain's mate holystoned the spar deck. The brass fittings and other bright metals were polished. The metal tracks on which the pivot guns were turned were burnished. The guns were cleaned. The rigging and blocks were checked. Once the ship was cleaned, the sailors washed themselves, some also shaved, with salt water. Following breakfast, or around 9:30 a.m., came the "call to quarters" when the guns were inspected and secured, ready for any emergency. The remainder of the day was spent in drill and performing the duties associated with sailing and maintaining the ship. The entry in Midshipman Blake's journal is likely an accurate description of a typical day's routine from an officer's perspective, "I have been quite busy all day, drilling the gun crews in the morning."[5]

There was plenty of hard work to be done. The two capstans, one each on the spar and gun decks, turned on the same axle. They were used for tasks that required great physical effort, like weighing anchor, and lifting boats and spars. When weighing the anchor, for example, a rope called the messenger formed a loop running from the capstan forward to the bows of the ship and back around the capstan. Bars then were inserted into the slots on the capstan's head. A detail of sailors would push the bars as they moved around the capstan. As the capstan turned, it would lock into place. While some men turned the capstan, others formed a relay to fasten the anchor cable to the messenger with short lengths of line called nippers. They followed the cable aft and quickly detached it as the cable went below to the cable tier. The men then returned to the bows to repeat the process until the anchor cable was completely stowed.

The bilge pump was used to remove water that accumulated in the ship's bilge. Located directly over the deepest part of the ship, the machine was worked by a crew of eight men. The water was then allowed to flow across the gun deck to the scuppers and into the sea.

Not all the shipboard tasks required sheer muscle alone. Some required great skill that only came with experience, like manning the helm. The helm consisted of a wheel at each end of a drum. Upon the drum were wound five and a half turns of rope, with a staple securing the midpoint to the drum. As the wheel was turned, the lines would move the tiller, which in turn controlled the rudder. Each spoke in the wheel corresponded to a certain angle of the rudder. The uppermost central spoke was specially shaped so it could be identified easily by feel in the hands of the helmsman, especially at night. Steering the ship was entrusted only to veteran seamen, and only a few in any ship's company had a "feel" for the job. They were assigned to the Master's department, and worked to attain petty officer rank with the rating of Quarter Master. A ship the size of *Constellation* required at least three quarter masters on duty at any time, including one at the "conn" who helped the master direct the movement of the ship.[6]

Helmsmen steered the ship with the use of the compass. The compass headings, given as directions such as "north by east," determined the course of the vessel. In a sailing ship, progress as well as direction was affected by the wind, and the helmsman had to compensate. The compass was placed in a housing called a binnacle, and contained a lamp for navigating at night. Compasses were placed in pairs so that even a single helmsman could always have one in view.

Not all work was performed on the spar and gun decks. The lowest deck is the orlop. Although out of sight from most of the crew, it was no place for loafing. As Midshipman Blake said, "I am to take charge of the hold and spirit room . . . I shall have rather more to do."[7] Used for storage, the forward and after orlop decks were lined with equipment storerooms for the various working departments of the ship and for stowing supplies. The bread lockers, for example, were lined with lead to help prevent infestation by pests and spoilage from dampness. Between the two sections of deck was the hold, where bulk supplies, cordage, chain, and canvas were stored after they were lowered through the main hatch. Across the hold were the tanks where water for cooking and drinking was stored. Gunpowder was kept in magazines and exploding projectiles were stored in shell rooms below the orlop deck, deep in the ship. To prevent explosion, lamps were placed in reflective lead-lined boxes with glass windows to provide light in these compartments. The vessel had to carry enough equipment, supplies, provisions, and ammunition to sustain itself and fight at sea for months at a time. As Yeoman Safford once recorded, "A large amount of cordage is being received in my Store Room, mostly manila for braces, etc. I am completely filled up. Enough provisions and stores have been taken aboard for six months." Accounting for all this property was the job of the yeoman. Reporting directly to the Executive Officer, he stored, issued, and maintained the books for supplies used by the various departments of the ship.[8]

Unlike the Army, the Navy employed men with the full-time rating of cook, and on some ships the men received three hot meals a day. Cooks prepared the meals at the Galley on the forward gun deck. They did not do all the work, however, and were assisted by mess cooks or cook's helpers.[9]

Each sailor was assigned to a mess, or team of men who ate meals together. A typical mess consisted of eight to fourteen men of the same rank and watch. Petty officers and marines messed separately, while the boys were distributed among the teams. Each member of the mess took his turn as orderly or mess cook. The mess cook, sometimes also called the caterer, unlocked the mess chest, took out the cooking utensils and tableware, and drew the food from the ship's cook or paymaster. A square of canvas was then placed over the mess team's table, and the men ate. Each member of the mess was responsible for keeping his own knife, fork, spoon, and cup and bucket. After the meal, the dishes were cleaned and returned to the mess chest, and the table was secured out of the way. Being mess cook was not a duty the men enjoyed, as Yeoman Safford's diary entry suggests, "I relinquished the catership of my mess today. It is quite a relief to be free of the duty."[10] Officers messed in the wardroom. They purchased their own food, which may have been a little better in quality than that of the men. Their food was prepared by the officers' cook and served by wardroom stewards or boys. The captain took his meals in his cabin, served by his steward, and he occasionally invited other officers to join him.

The morning meal typically consisted of one pint of coffee, hardtack or ship's biscuit, and a piece of salted junk (hard, salted beef). Lunch was the main meal of the day and could include a piece of cooked beef or pork, dried vegetables or beans, biscuit, maybe some cheese, and coffee. The various messes were usually served light fare again in the evening, and, as with all meals, at times determined by the watch schedules.

It could take some time to get used to shipboard larder. Safford described the corned beef as "the worse kind of horse," and the mackerel as "rusty fish," both of which required the men to drink "such quantities of water as is required to freshen them sufficiently for the digestion to function after they are eaten." Even the water did not escape notice. Stored in iron tanks, it was said to look like "some kind of liquor for coloring red"; and was probably why coffee was a popular beverage. The menu at sea could get monotonous. When in port or on coastal blockade duty, however, the paymaster and cooks took advantage of the opportunity to obtain fresh provisions. Yeoman Safford recorded an oft-repeated ritual in his diary saying, "As soon as we dropped anchor a boat was sent ashore for bread and vegetables. Word of our needs must have been passed ashore for we are being surrounded with boats bringing bread and fruit to sell."[11] On special occasions when they were in port, the paymaster would issue each mess additional money to purchase extra food or special items for a holiday meal, such as turkeys at Thanksgiving and Christmas.

Ships of *Constellation*'s class were authorized a medical staff consisting of three doctors; one Surgeon and two Assistant or Passed Assistant Surgeons. They were assisted by one petty officer rated as a Surgeon's Steward, and three sailors assigned as Nurses. A Boy could also be assigned to work in the Surgeon's department. The medical officers treated a variety of illnesses from common colds to typhus; conditions of exhaustion and seasickness; injuries caused by the physical strain and hazards associated with sailing; and maladies, like scurvy, attributed to poor shipboard diets. Liberal in their dispensing of drugs, surgeons prescribed a variety of medicines to control fevers, or help purge the body of bad fluids; although some were not very effective. Sailors did not report for Sick Call on a lark, as Yeoman Safford commented, "I do not like to patronize the Dispensary. One is usually better off without their drugs."[12]

Those too infirm to perform normal duties were placed on the Sick List and confined in the Sick Bay, located on the forward berth deck, until they recovered. Safford described one of the occasions he submitted to the surgeon's care saying, "I was suddenly taken sick with severe pains in my body, which soon made me extremely weak. I made my way as best I could to the sick bay, was put on the 'sick list' and remained in a hammock all day."[13] In battle, casualties were treated below in a surgeon's station established in the cockpit, near the after orlop.[14] Flying wood splinters and metal shrapnel caused most casualties in nineteenth-century naval battles, and frequently, the only way to save a man's life was to amputate a mangled limb. When the illness or injury was beyond the capability of the ship's surgeon to treat, the patient was normally transferred to a hospital at a Navy Yard or base. Safford recorded one such occurrence in 1863 when he wrote, "We put three men on an American bark to be taken to the Naval Hospital in New York."[15]

Dentistry was coming into its own as a medical art during the Civil War, but not all dentists had received professional training. Many Civil War sailors sought help from naval surgeons whose kits may have contained some dental instruments. Sailors also sought dental treatment from other practitioners in the various ports they visited. Safford described one woman who came on board at Spezia, Italy as "an admirable operator" after she removed the remains of two broken teeth.[16] The men of *Constellation* were also fortunate in having such a practitioner as a shipmate. "A tooth has been troubling me for several days," Safford recounted. "Our marine barber and dentist, Edsall, extracted it. He did the job well."[17] No mention is recorded of his tonsorial skill, however.

If a sailor died during a cruise, his remains were not shipped home for burial. If one died while in port, the deceased was buried in a nearby cemetery. If at sea, a man's body was wrapped in his hammock, weighted down with a 32-pound shot each at the head and foot, and committed to the deep with an appropriate memorial ceremony. Safford recorded the proceedings of the first sea burial of the Civil War cruise, which he called "an impressive sight to witness," by saying, "All hands were called to bury the dead . . . [A] round the dead sailor . . . were congregated his shipmates with uncovered heads. They listened to a reading from the Testament by the First Lieutenant." Describing another burial a year later, he wrote, "After reading the usual service, the body was slid from the lee gangway into the sea, there to remain, while his shipmates whom he has left behind resumed their duties about the ship . . . with careless indifference."[18]

Although Chaplains were only posted to flagships in the Civil War, the spiritual needs of the men on other vessels were not neglected. On Sunday mornings, following General Muster and the weekly Captain's Inspection, the commander or one of the officers would lead the crew in Divine Services on the spar deck, when weather permitted. Customarily the service included the reading of prayers or scripture.[19] One Sunday each month, after religious worship, a commissioned officer also read An Act for the Better Government of the Navy to the assembled crew.

Commonly called the "Navy Regulations," this new law was approved by President Lincoln on 17 July 1862. An improvement over the old Articles of War, it did away with the practice of "tricing-up" offenders. After the Congress abolished flogging without giving guidance for a substitute in 1850, some officers and masters-at-arms turned to tricing up, where offenders were tied with their hands behind the backs, and suspended from beams with their feet just off the gun deck.[20] Safford likened it to crucifixion, saying it was "in my opinion worse than flogging in the old Navy."[21] As a lawyer in civilian life, he probably welcomed the new regulation that included guidelines specifying the punishment allowed for particular violations, and who had authority to impose what punishment.

The most severe cases were heard by courts-martial, consisting of boards of at least five officers appointed by a squadron commander holding flag rank. Courts Martial could impose any punishment, including death, long prison sentences and forfeiture of all pay. Article 10 allowed a ship's commanding officer authority to impose limited punishment to members of his crew for minor infractions and to maintain good order and discipline. A captain could also delegate some authority to junior officers for treating lesser offenses. Both courts-martial and commanding officers had authority to reduce sailors in rank for certain violations. They could also confine offenders in the brig, place them in wrist and leg irons, and reduce rations to bread and water for short periods. Offenders could also be restricted to the vessel when in port, or given extra police or fatigue duties around the ship. *Constellation*'s brig was located on the forward orlop deck.[22]

To insure that justice was served, Yeoman Safford was often appointed to practice his legal skills as defense counsel. One case that he lost involved two members of the Marine Guard. Musician James McNamara was accused of theft. Private Michael Gaul was charged as his accomplice and tried separately.[23] After an attempt to have the charges dismissed failed, McNamara was found guilty and sentenced to thirty days confinement in double irons, loss of three months pay, and extra police duty for a like period. Captain Stellwagen, however, refused to accept the decision on the grounds he thought the evidence insufficient.[24] Gaul was not so lucky. Contrary to his expectations, Safford wrote, "Gaul's Court Martial sentence was announced at muster. He is to lose three month's pay, be confined for thirty days in the brig in double irons on bread and water, and to perform three month's extra police duty after his release."[25] The commanding officer approved the sentence.

Despite the rigors of navy life and discipline, the members of the crew enjoyed a variety of diversions. Sunday afternoons, when in port, were generally reserved for "loafing," and there was some time for recreation when the watch and training schedules allowed. During this personal time, sailors and marines usually wrote letters, read books or newspapers, or just relaxed and dozed. Some passed time repairing or adding decorative needlework to their clothing, or played games like checkers and dominos. Cards were forbidden, but undoubtedly found their way on board. Gambling was not allowed, but went on behind the officers' backs. Favorite games of chance included calling "odds and evens," rolling dice or betting wagers on daily activities. Safford described one example of an activity that captured much attention during the observance of Independence Day in 1863. "I went ashore," he wrote, "and witnessed amid great excitement a boat race between our fourth and fifth cutters. The fourth cutter won." One can only guess if some of the excitement was due to bets that may have been wagered on the outcome.[26]

Members of the crew staged minstrel or theatrical shows, or played musical instruments. Midshipman Blake took time to enjoy some homespun music, as one of his journal entries read:

> I went over and spent a musical night with the master's mates tonight. One of them plays the guitar, another the bones, and [Paymaster] Pangborn was there as grave as a judge, beating the tambourine. This combination would make rather rough music, were it not for one of the wardroom boys who fiddles quite well, and adds his mite to the harmony of the occasion.[27]

Others staged boxing and wrestling matches, contests of skill, or engaged in horseplay. Those who wished to smoke went to the forecastle. There, they lit their pipes or cigars from an easily extinguished taper from whale or olive oil "smoking lamps." Friction matches were forbidden because of the danger of fire. Some men told and listened to yarns, or just relaxed in the fresh air before going below deck to sleep in the stifling air of the berth deck.

One of the most anticipated activities was pay call. After being inspected in his best uniform by his leading petty officers and officers, a sailor reported to the paymaster. If he did not owe the government any money for lost items of equipment or clothing, and had no balance on his account in the ship's small store, he could collect his month's wages. In 1863 Seamen were paid $18 per month; Ordinary Seamen $14; Landsmen and other inexperienced hands $12; and First, Second, and Third Class Boys $9, $8, and $7, respectively. Petty officers could earn up to $35 per month depending on rating and length of service. To compensate for the abolition of the grog (a rum or whisky and water beverage) ration in 1862, the men over the age of twenty-one received an additional $1.50 each month. The Marine Corps pay structure differed somewhat. The Orderly Sergeant received $24 per month; Sergeants $20; Corporals $18; and Musicians and Privates $16. When at sea, the marines also received an additional $1.50 sea pay.

Yeoman Safford recalled, "When sailors get hold of money they believe in putting it into circulation immediately."[28] Therefore, the favorite recreation activities for the crew began with the sounding of liberty call. Few activities were more popular or memorable than liberty, or a pass to go ashore to escape the usual routine. The commanding officer usually allowed half the crew to go on liberty at any one time, and there was stiff punishment for those who remained ashore after their passes expired.

When in port, *Constellation's* men took the opportunity to get away from the tedium of shipboard life. They dined in fine restaurants, slept in comfortable hotel beds, purchased souvenirs and tailor-made clothes for themselves and the folks back home, had their photographs taken, attended the religious worship services of their choice, and did some sight seeing. Some sought romance or more casual female companionship. With the abolition of the grog ration and prohibition against any "spirituous liquor" on board U.S. naval vessels in 1862, some members of the crew went on quests for alcoholic beverages. A few ran into trouble with local authorities, overstayed their passes and ran afoul of the captain, or both. On the whole, though, *Constellation's* men were well behaved.

Frequently local families, dignitaries, and the American Consul would host balls and dances, extending invitations to the officers and men of visiting ships. Midshipman Blake confided one such occurrence in Naples to his diary. "One of the ladies invited me to her house to a dance on Tuesday evening, to which I think I shall go."[29] The captain and officers of *Constellation* returned the hospitality by entertaining local residents on board. Yeoman Safford described one such soiree in Marseilles, "The Captain and the First Lieutenant returned from the city with a party of ladies who are entertained at a luncheon after which there is a dance on the spar deck."[30]

Even more than a soldier in the field, a sailor or marine at sea was isolated, and cut off from news at home for months at a time. When not relaxing or engaging in some leisure activity, almost everyone's thoughts turned to those they left behind. Many of the men carried and cherished photographs of their loved ones, but mail was their real link to home. Like military members of any era, receiving mail was the highlight of one's day, week, or even month. As Yeoman Safford put it, "This morning I received a letter from home. No letter ever came to me with a more hearty welcome."[31] Midshipman Blake's journal shows that officers and enlisted men alike shared such thoughts, when he wrote, "I received a nice long letter from home and another from my friend Miss L. Both were just as welcome as they could be."[32]

Knowing its impact on morale, the Navy did its best to get mail to and from the men using supply vessels that brought provisions to the deployed ships and through the American Consulates or naval stations in foreign ports. Many sailors spent their free time writing, reading, and re-reading letters. Despite the efforts of the service, it was not uncommon for men to receive word from home that a child had been born, or that a beloved family member had died many months before. There was particular concern for friends and relatives serving in the Army on bloody fields with names like Antietam and Gettysburg.

At 8:00 p.m. (or 9:00 when the sun set after 6:00) "Tattoo" was sounded by the boatswain's pipe. The hammocks were removed from the rails in preparation for sleep by the watch off-duty, followed by the call for "lights out."[33]

Landsman Emmet Barnes, ship's No. 235, photographed wearing the tailored suit he purchased while on liberty in Italy in 1864.

The crew could be called to quarters any time, day or night. (U.S. Naval Historical Center)

CHAPTER 7

FIGHTING ON A MAN-OF-WAR

"WE WERE NOT IN READINESS FOR ACTION. WE DEMONSTRAT-ed the lack of drill."[1] Yeoman Safford's comment early in the cruise probably understated the obvious. Although there were some seasoned hands on board when *Constellation* left Portsmouth Navy Yard in March 1862, her crew was not yet fully trained. One of the duties of the captain, therefore, was to transform the collection of veterans and recruits that constituted the ship's company into an efficient team. He did this by scheduling formal training, regular practices, and surprise exercises. The men soon learned what was required in working the great guns and boat howitzers, handling small arms, pikes and cutlasses, and manning the boats. They had to be ready to execute hasty repairs of battle damage, fight fires, and keep the ship afloat while continuing to sail the vessel and fight. In addition, they had to be proficient in executing tactics that would enable them to fight "by land and sea" in order to project the fleet's power. Every man had to know his assigned duty, as well as those of several comrades in the event they became casualties. The survival of the ship and men depended on it.[2]

Training the crew was no easy task, as Midshipman Blake attested early in his journal when he wrote, "I have been quite busy all day, drilling the gun crews. . . . Rather up hill work . . . ."[3] The sailors were not the only ones who were green. Yeoman Safford probably expressed the opinion of many "old salts," and may have been referring to Blake, when he wrote, "What a bore to be drilled by one like the midshipman in command of our Division, whose proficiency is acquired entirely from reading a book just prior to the drill."[4] To prevent monotony and improve readiness for action, the captain would vary the training sequences, so that no two days' schedules were alike. Drills were called at any time. Midshipman Blake recalled one surprise drill, "Last night we had general quarters. The captain went himself and called the music, and not a soul but himself knew that we were to have them before the drum beat."[5]

As in the modern Navy, "General Quarters" was the alarm to man their battle stations and prepare the ship to fight. With the sounds of the drum roll, alarm rattles, boatswains' whistles, and shouted order for "all hands prepare ship for action," men ceased routine activity or sprang from their sleep to perform those duties that their training had made second nature. Yeoman Safford described the scene from a petty officer's perspective: "General Quarters. . . . At the roll of the drum out of their hammocks came the watch below; then begins the general scramble." Each man knew his station and reported there immediately, as Safford commented, "I was the first man to report to the officer of my station . . . being in the 5th Division at the Starboard Shell Room."[6]

In battle, a warship's main strength was found in her "great guns." *Constellation*'s main battery, located on the gun deck, consisted of twenty cannon mounted on naval four-truck carriages. This armament gave her a broadside of ten guns each to port and starboard: eight 8-inch Navy chambered shell guns flanked by two 32-pounder solid shot firing long guns.

The gun deck of a ship like USS *Constellation* in action. (U.S. Naval Historical Center)

An 8-inch shell gun, served by a crew of 14 men and a powder boy, could fire a 51.5 pound exploding shell to a range of 2,300 yards with a 9.7-second time of flight, using a 9 pound powder charge and 10° of muzzle elevation. The same charge at 5° of elevation fired a 52-pound shrapnel shell 1,600 yards with a 5.8-second time of flight. The 32-pounders were each served by a crew of 12 men and a powder boy. Also using a 9-pound powder cartridge and 10° of barrel elevation, these guns fired a 32-pound solid iron cannon ball 2,731 yards with a 10.7-second time of flight.[7]

Each gun crew was responsible for a pair of guns, one on the port side, and its "opposite number" on the starboard. The gun crews were then grouped into two divisions, each with four 8-inch and one 32-pounder gun crews. A lieutenant, who was assisted by a midshipman, commanded each division. A quarter gunner, who saw to the readiness of the guns and their paraphernalia, was also assigned to each division. The First Division, located on the forward gun deck, was commanded by the first, or senior, lieutenant, followed aft by the Second Division, commanded by the next ranking line officer, the second lieutenant. Each gun crew had an even number of men, designated First and Second for each critical position, with titles reflective of their duties, plus a powder boy. The captains of the guns gave the commands, primed, aimed and fired the weapons. The spongers swabbed the tubes to extinguish burning embers, and rammed home the new cartridges and projectiles. The loaders placed the cartridges and projectiles in the muzzle, and assisted the spongers in ramming them home. The shot- or shellmen procured the projectiles and wadding, and passed them to the loaders. The handspikemen raised the breech of the gun so the quoin could be moved to adjust the elevation of the muzzle. The remainder of the men were the train and side tacklemen who hauled on the ropes that ran the guns in and out, and adjusted direction left and right. If the first sponger became disabled, for example, the second sponger would assume his duties. If the ship had to fight on both sides, the first captain, sponger and loader would man one gun, while the seconds served its opposite number, and the remaining were designated as shifting men, moving between the two to serve both.[8]

Located on the top, or spar deck and mounted on pivot carriages, was a secondary battery of two rifled cannon that formed the Third Division. The pivot mounts permitted these guns to fire at greater elevations than the gun ports on the gun deck allowed, and with fewer crewmen. A 30-pound (4.2-inch) Parrott rifle was located on the forecastle, near the bow. Its barrel weighed 3,500 pounds and was served by a crew of nine, including a powder boy. When fired at 25º elevation with a 3.25-pound powder charge, the 29-pound shell had a maximum range of 6,700 yards with a 27-second time of flight. A 20-pound (3.67-inch) Parrott rifle was located at the stern. Its barrel weighed 1,700 pounds, and was served by a crew of seven, including a powder boy. When fired at 15º of elevation, a 2-pound powder charge propelled a 19-pound shell 4,400 yards with a 17.25-second time of flight, or a 19-pound shrapnel (case shot) 950 yards in 1.12 seconds. The pivot mount, on which each Parrot was placed, consisted of a bed that held the gun, a slide that absorbed the recoil, and training trucks (or caster wheels) that traversed metal tracks on the deck. This allowed the rifle to pivot into different firing positions.[9]

Constellation had additional armament with three 12-pound Dahlgren bronze boat howitzers: two heavy, one light. These weapons were used in the ship's boats to pursue and attack enemy vessels in shallow water, attack other small boats, cover the landing of troops, or be landed by seamen and marines for shore operations. The heavy barrel model weighed 750 pounds, and the light 430 pounds. Each had a crew of eight men, and was mounted in

Union Sailors drilling with a boat howitzer on its field carriage. (U.S. Naval Historical Center)

the bow of a launch on a boat carriage that allowed 120° traverse without changing the vessel's course. When landing on shore, the crew could mount the piece on its field carriage in three minutes or less. The field carriage, weighing nearly 500 pounds, was made entirely of wrought iron and was hauled by sailors using a drag rope. A small wheel at the end of the trail eased movement and was turned up when firing. An anti-personnel weapon for close combat, howitzers fired exploding shell, shrapnel or spherical case, and canister munitions (but not solid shot). A one-pound powder charge propelled a 10-pound shell for 1,085 yards, or a 13-pound shrapnel shell 1,150 yards. A well-drilled crew could fire three or four rounds per minute; although seven or eight per minute was possible in extreme circumstances. In an emergency, the field carriage-mounted howitzers could also be used on the spar deck.[10]

While the gun crews reported to their guns and prepared them for firing, the rest of the ship's company were reporting to their stations. The Fourth Division was also known as the Master's Division. It was composed of twenty-four enlisted men who were stationed in the tops and on deck who attended the rigging, sails, steering, and signals. The executive officer, who was second in command, controlled the division in combat from the quarterdeck, with the assistance of the master. This arrangement enabled the executive officer to assume command immediately in case the captain was disabled and prevented any confusion or delay in the passing of sailing orders. The boatswain assisted the master from a position on the forecastle. The assignment of the line officers to divisions by their descending order of seniority placed a less experienced lieutenant close to the quarterdeck, where he could be observed, supervised, and mentored by the executive officer. The captain also posted himself on the quarterdeck where he could best observe and control the ship and action.[11]

A midshipman usually commanded the Fifth Division, also called the Powder Division. It provided the gun crews with ammunition and consisted mostly of men from departments whose routine duties were below deck. The gunner took charge of the main or forward magazine and supervised the preparation of powder cartridges there and of shells and fuses in the shell rooms. The gunner's mate assisted from the smaller aft magazine and shot locker. Three chains of sailors would pass the cartridges in leather passing boxes upward through scuttles to the gun deck where waiting powder boys carried them to their guns. The empty passing boxes were then sent back to the magazines through canvas chutes where they were reloaded and the process was repeated. The projectiles were placed in wooden boxes and hoisted up through hatches to the gun and spar decks using shell whips. After they were unloaded and the shot placed in racks and shells in boxes near the appropriate guns, the empty boxes were returned below and reloaded in a continuous process. The officer in charge of the Powder Division also saw that the means for lowering the wounded below and conveying them to the surgeon's station were in place and functioning.[12]

The carpenter's and sail maker's departments reported to the Powder Division's officer, but worked under the direction of their respective warrant officers. They first removed stanchions and bulkheads and placed gratings over the open hatches to facilitate handling the guns and minimize the effects of flying splinters. They then secured all portholes, prepared the pumps for controlling leaks, rigged the fire engine and checked the flood cocks. During battle they stood by with plugs and patches to repair shot holes, clear wreckage and fight fires. The master-at-arms and ship's corporals extinguished galley fires and all unauthorized lights; and insured the safe use of lamps. They also had loose gunpowder quickly swept from the deck or dumped from passing boxes over tubs of water to prevent accidental ignition.[13]

The surgeon (or senior medical officer on board), along with his assistant surgeons,

Surgeon's Station in the cockpit during battle. (U.S. Army Military History Institute)

steward (petty officer) and nurses (lower enlisted men) of the Surgeon's Division established an aid station in the cockpit, a section of the hold below the waterline. They also prepared tourniquets for controlling the bleeding of the wounded and distributed them to the various divisions. The paymaster secured the money, books, and stores in the wardroom while his steward safeguarded the property in his custody in his office compartment; and kept an eye on the spirit room as well.[14]

The Division of Marines formed ranks on the quarterdeck, loaded their muskets and fixed bayonets. Under the command of their lieutenant, they stood by to execute the captain's orders to fire into the opposing ship, repel boarders, man cannons, or lead an assault that would take the fight to the enemy.[15]

Pistols, cutlasses, muskets, boarding pikes, and battleaxes were distributed to sailors from the armory. Each man knew his position and function in the event of any contingency. In addition to their duties on the guns, each member of a gun crew was designated as a member of either the First or Second Division of Boarders. In a close-in fight, the second half of the gun crew of each piece, and all petty officers on the spar deck (except the quartermasters at the wheel and on the conn) were first boarders armed with pistols and cutlasses. The first half of each gun crew was designated as the second boarders. When the order to "Board the Enemy" was given, the broadside guns continued to fire with depressed elevations to damage the enemy's gun deck and hull. The spar deck rifles were loaded with grapeshot and howitzers with canister to sweep the enemy's deck. The marines and musket equipped seamen fired at visible enemy personnel. Following a hail of gunfire and musketry, the borders attacked![16]

If an enemy attempted to board *Constellation*, the order to "Prepare to Repel Boarders" would be given to defend the ship. One fourth of the men in each gun crew, and the remainder of the master's division, except those designated as boarders or on the wheel, were assigned as pikemen. The pikemen formed behind those crewmen armed with cutlasses. The marines, with bayonets fixed, formed behind the pikemen to cover them. At the command "Repel Boarders," grape and musketry was brought to bear upon the enemy as they prepared to attack. Men remaining on the broadside guns continued to fire and stood by with pikes to repel any enemy attempting to enter through the gun ports or quarter galleries. The howitzers, charged with canister, stood ready should the enemy gain a foothold on the spar deck. When the fighting became desperate enough to call all hands from below, the pikemen took up muskets and left their pikes for the members of the powder division to use as they came on deck.[17]

One member of each gun crew was designated a fireman, and equipped with a firebucket and battleaxe to extinguish flames and clear wreckage. All members of the spar deck gun crews, except the first captains, first spongers, first loaders, and powder boys, were also assigned as sailtrimmers. Besides reinforcing the master's division in trimming sails, they also supplemented the firemen and pumpmen, or assembled to be armed with muskets for use as a landing force; they were usually crewmembers of the ship's boats. Each gun crew also furnished one pumpman.[18]

Captain Stellwagen and his men expected to fight the steamer *Southerner*, which they believed had already been delivered to the Confederate States Navy in European waters.

In combat, *Constellation*'s Marine Guard would have worn uniforms like the marines pictured at the Washington Navy Yard in 1861. (U.S. Naval Historical Center)

The rebel ship was reportedly armed with Armstrong rifled guns, which could out-range all *Constellation*'s guns except the 30-pounder Parrott. To have any chance against this supposed superior enemy ship, Stellwagen's only hope was to approach close enough to disable *Southerner* with long-range fire before she could steam to windward, where *Constellation* could not follow. *Constellation* could then close to where her crew's superior skill at gunnery and the weight of her broadside would send the Confederate commerce raider "where she ought to be," or board and capture her. Moses Safford wrote that Gunner John Grainger had "showed remarkable results at target practice" with the 30-pounder, and the captain ordered him to personally take charge of that gun. This extraordinary assignment left Yeoman Safford in charge of the forward magazine, the gunner's regular station.[19]

Gunner John R. Grainger.

The number, type, and frequency of drills were vital to the ship's defense and the survival of the crew. The realism that went into the training enhanced the crew's motivation and ability. The constant drilling, day and night, molded the crew into a well-trained unit as it developed into an efficient fighting team. Yeoman Safford remarked, "Our men have been doing some really extraordinary work at target practice." As their proficiency grew, he added, "Both our Captain and Executive have the confidence of the men." As an ultimate testament to their readiness, while recognizing the limitations of their vessel, Safford proudly proclaimed, "Our men were very eager for a fight. I do not know what we could have done with a steam ship, but before she [the enemy ship] had finished us they [the enemy sailors] would have known they were in a fight!"[20]

USS *Constellation* circa 1871, after conversion to a sail and gunnery practice ship for the U.S. Naval Academy. (U.S. Naval Historical Center)

CHAPTER 8

PRACTICE AND TRAINING SHIP

FOLLOWING HER CIVIL WAR SERVICE, AND A BRIEF STINT AS A Receiving Ship at Norfolk and Philadelphia, the Navy's leadership recognized *Constellation's* usefulness as a floating classroom for the U.S. Naval Academy at Annapolis, Maryland. Although the Navy was converting to steam propulsion and iron ships, the all-sail, all wooden ship was recognized as an ideal platform for teaching the effects of wind and tide, practical seamanship, navigation, and ship management to the Navy's future officers. To accommodate a complement of midshipmen and a small regular crew, the ship was modified with additional cabins on the after gun and berth decks, and wash rooms and water closets on the forward gun and berth decks. The brig was enlarged by converting the bread rooms into cells and subdividing the existing cells on the forward orlop deck. The shell rooms beneath the forward orlop deck were converted to coal storage. *Constellation* departed Annapolis on her first training cruise in June of 1871. For the next twenty-two years she would be placed in commission every spring, embark with midshipmen in June, return to Annapolis by September; and decommissioned every winter.[1]

During the winter of 1871–1872 *Constellation* was further modified for training midshipmen in naval gunnery. She received a main battery of eight 9-inch Dahlgren guns, four on each side of the gun deck. Between each pair of 9-inch guns was a larger caliber weapon on a pivot mount; an 11-inch Dahlgren gun and a 100-pounder Parrott rifle on the port and starboard sides, respectively. To accommodate these huge guns, the number four gun ports on each side were widened to a width of ten feet. Sometime during the 1870s *Constellation* was also given a navigating bridge over the spar deck.[2]

The midshipmen's training cruises took *Constellation* up the coast of the United States to New England, down to Saint Thomas in the Virgin Islands, or across the Atlantic to Europe. The cruise of 1874, under the command of Civil War veteran Captain Kidder Breese, was typical. One midshipman who embarked on his Third Class, or sophomore year, summer practice cruise that year was Herbert O. Dunn. Born in Westerly, Rhode Island, he was appointed to the Naval Academy in June 1873. He kept a detailed notebook of the gunnery and seamanship instruction, as well as an account of a visit to the grave of Napoleon on the island of St. Helena. The entries in the Academy's Conduct Book show that he was reported for minor infractions such as missing muster, not wearing a collar at supper formation, wearing a torn working suit, and "skylarking" (daydreaming) while on the cruise. After graduating in June 1879, he served on active duty in the U.S. Navy, and rose to the rank of Rear Admiral before retiring in 1921.[3]

His distinguished career included command of USS *Terror* during the Spanish-American War, the battleship USS *Idaho* in the "Great White Fleet (1909–1911), and the U.S. naval base in the Azores during World War I (1918–1919). In addition, he served as a junior officer aboard the cruiser USS *Baltimore* (1889–1892) and in shore assignments at Baltimore, Maryland as officer in charge of the Navy Hydrographic Office (1892–1895, and again

Small arms drill on board USS _Constellation_ circa 1884. (U.S. Naval Historical Center)

1898–1900) and the Naval Recruiting Station (1905–1906, and again 1907–1909). He invented the Dunn Anchor in 1889, which became the standard on U.S. Navy ships. Admiral Dunn died in Baltimore on 13 February 1930. Not every midshipman who trained on board _Constellation_ became a flag officer, but every future flag officer that attended the Naval Academy from 1871 to 1893 trained on _Constellation_.[4]

From March to July 1878 the annual training cruise was delayed while the ship transported exhibits to France for the Paris Exposition and delivered stores to the Mediterranean Squadron. At about the time she was visiting French ports, it seems that many people began to think she was the frigate namesake converted to a sloop-of-war in 1853–1854, instead of a different ship with the same name. Following the midshipmen's practice cruise of 1879, the vessel departed Annapolis under the command of Captain John Davis to carry supplies to the Mediterranean Squadron. Instead of returning to Annapolis, as was her custom, _Constellation_ went into the New York Navy Yard in early 1880. There, she was readied for a mission of mercy.

In March 1880 she was commissioned to take supplies obtained by the Irish Relief Fund to help alleviate the suffering from a famine. _Constellation_'s armament and some ballast were removed and carpenters built bins in the hold and on the orlop deck in which to

Top: Loading famine relief supplies on
board *Constellation* in New York, 1880.

Bottom: U.S. Officers and Irish dignitaries on board
Constellation in 1880. (U.S. Naval Historical Center)

stow the humanitarian cargo. She departed New York under the command of Captain Edward E. Potter, USN, on 27 March carrying over 2,500 barrels of potatoes and flour. Upon arrival off Queenstown on 20 April, her cargo was off-loaded onto lighters for delivery to the people of Ireland.[5] For delivering these relief supplies, and possibly to embarrass the British government politically, the Lord Mayor presented a proclamation "From the People of the County and City of Cork," that read as follows:

> To **Captain Potter**, the Officers and Crew of the American Naval Ship **Constellation**.
> On the threshold of that **Country** you have come to succour [sic] on a sad mission of noble charity we greet you warmly and welcome you and proffer the gratitude sincere indeed of a poor down-trodden but **liberty loving people**.
> The desire to express our gratefulness to the generous citizens of your **Free Country** for the many practical manifestations of sympathy with our suffering people and to your **Government** for the promptitude shown by giving the Gallant Ship under your command for the transmission here of your timely relief.
> In return for such noble and unselfish generosity we can only hope that in future generations as it has been in the immediate past that **Irishmen** will be ever ready to defend **America's** honor and **Integrity** and continue to be the vigilant sentinels on the watchtowers of her liberties.
> In conclusion we can only say that that **Flag** which is the epitomization [sic] of your **Country's** honoured history the **Spangled** diploma of your well won authority will be ever respected by those who have been afforded by a melancholy coincidence the opportunity of seeing you here today. **God Save Ireland** (emphasis from the original).[6]

After taking on additional ballast to compensate for the lightened load, the ship sailed for home on 11 May. A month later, she was back in Annapolis. Following a week of preparations, she departed on her annual cruise to train the U.S. Navy's future officers.

During the *Constellation*'s stay at Annapolis, the academy made the transition from a  "marlinspike" seamanship to a steam navigation school. Under the forward thinking naval educator, Captain Stephen B. Luce, the academy assumed the status of a good university, with graduates qualified to sail and fight steel ships, and to lead the technicians who would man the "New Navy" of the 1890s. Cadet Midshipmen still trained in marksmanship and seamanship, as usual, but the days of the annual sailing

Midshipmen on board USS *Constellation* circa 1886.
(U.S. Naval Historical Center)

60

Midshipmen furling sail on the Monkey Yard circa 1893. (U.S. Naval Historical Center)

practice cruise were drawing to a close. Before ending her days at the Naval Academy *Constellation* was employed for one more special mission. Under the command of Captain Caspar F. Goodrich from September 1892 to February 1893, *Constellation* transported works of art from Europe to New York for the Columbian Exposition in Chicago. She departed on her final training cruise to the Azores and Canary Islands on 3 June 1893, returning under sail for the last time on 29 August. While waiting for the tug to take her to her berth, she once again rendered assistance to a stricken vessel. The entry in *Constellation*'s deck log read, "sent a life boat to a wreck astern and rescued Captain A. E. Morse and Seaman W. E. Beechum of the disabled schooner *Sudex* of Annapolis, which had dragged her anchor and knocked a hole in her by going through [A] wharf." On 2 September 1893, she was placed out of commission as a Practice Ship for the last time at Annapolis.[7]

Commodore Stephen B. Luce, more than anyone else, brought the U.S. Navy into the age of steel. He did it by developing his vision for training the new Navy. After implementing this vision for training officers at the Naval Academy, he extended it to the training of enlisted men. He believed in adding exercises that challenged one's mental reflexes to the training objectives. Campaigning for sailors who could use their heads, Luce established the Naval Apprentice Training System and developed a similar school program for the Merchant Marine. Sailors were taught the "why," as well as the "what" and "how" as they "learned the ropes." *Constellation* was a natural choice for a vehicle to put the theory into practice.[8]

In September 1893, three weeks after returning from her last

USS *Constellation* under sail, circa 1893. (U.S. Naval Historical Center)

Training at Newport, Rhode Island on board *Constellation* circa 1915.

midshipmen's practice cruise, *Constellation* was towed to Norfolk for repair and preparation for her new assignment as a stationary training ship. Arriving under tow at Newport, Rhode Island on 22 May 1894, she remained a permanently moored vessel, except for two excursions and occasional trips to the repair yard. One such visit to the New York Navy Yard from June to December 1904 included a survey to determine her usefulness and desirability for repair. The survey report recommended that her repairs, though costly, should proceed not only because of her famous history but also because it was believed that excellent drills could be con-

ducted with her spars, rigging, and sails. *Constellation* resumed training naval apprentice seamen in January 1905 after receiving a new set of sails and running rigging. By July 1910, however, her complete inventory of sails and running rigging were condemned and were never to be replaced. Although recruits continued to exercise in the rig as part of their "boot camp" experience, training in sail handling had finally come to an end.[9]

By 1912, the belief that *Constellation* was the frigate namesake launched in Baltimore in 1797 had become widespread. An organization in that city, the National Star Spangled Banner Centennial Commission, began lobbying to have the ship participate in a celebration recognizing the one-hundredth anniversary of the writing of the song that became our national anthem. Wielding considerable political influence, the commission succeeded in having Acting Secretary of the Navy Franklin D. Roosevelt order a survey that found her in acceptable condition to be viewed by the public. Roosevelt ordered *Constellation* to be restored "as she appeared in 1814." To minimize the estimated costs required for full restoration, he stipulated that the work "include only such general details as would be noticed by the layman." The cosmetic work included fabricating twenty-two guns at the Boston Navy Yard, dummy sails stuffed

USS *Constellation* in Baltimore in 1914 for the Star Spangled Banner Centennial. (U.S. Naval Historical Center)

with straw, removal of the 1880s-era bridge platform and 1890s deck housing, and replacement of the two working iron capstans with one non-working wooden one. *Constellation* was ready for the pageantry.[10]

Towed to Baltimore harbor, *Constellation* was on display from 7 September (anniversary of the namesake frigate's launching) until 29 October 1914. She was then towed to Washington, D.C. where she was on display from 31 October to 4 December. After stopping in Norfolk for repairs in December, she returned to training duty at Newport. A recommendation by the Bureau of Construction and Repair that the ship be "stripped down to the lower masts and converted practically to a hulk" was rejected by the Navy Department with the response that "this historic vessel should be retained in her present form." When the Navy ended training in sail handling in July 1920, *Constellation* remained in Newport seeing decreased activity over the next twenty years, serving once more as a Receiving Ship to house naval recruits.[11]

The ship's official name was changed to *Old Constellation* on 30 October 1917 to prevent confusion in having two ships with the same name. In keeping with naval tradition of naming new ships after famous predecessors, a new battle cruiser under construction during World War I was christened *Constellation*. The sloop reverted to her original name on 24 July 1925 after the battle cruiser was scrapped under provisions of the Washington Naval Treaty.

Constellation made her last public appearance as a commissioned vessel to help commemorate the 150th anniversary of the United States Declaration of Independence on 4 July 1926. Early that year, the Chief of Naval Operations asked

USS *Constellation* at the Philadelphia Navy Yard in 1926. (U.S. Naval Historical Center)

that *Constellation* be made ready to take part in the festivities. On 15 May she was towed to Philadelphia and moored with the protected cruiser USS *Olympia*, Admiral Dewey's flagship at the 1898 battle of Manila Bay. Following the celebration and after a short period in dry-dock at the Philadelphia Navy Yard, she was towed back to Newport. Meanwhile, political efforts to move the vessel permanently to Baltimore were underway. On 16 June 1933 a Navy Department order placed *Constellation* in a decommissioned status for preservation as a naval relic. Although numerous surveys were conducted and estimates given for the cost of restoring the vessel as a national historic shrine, no decisions on the ship's fate were taken.[12]

On 24 August 1940 *Constellation* was recommissioned at Newport by order of President Franklin D. Roosevelt, and on 8 January 1941 she was given the designation "IX-20." On 21 May 1941, *Constellation* was designated the Relief (or standby) Flagship of Admiral Ernest J. King, Commander-in-Chief of the U.S. Atlantic Fleet. With King's appointment as Chief of Naval Operations at the beginning of America's involvement in World War II, *Constellation* continued in this capacity, and alternately as relief flagship for the Atlantic Fleet's Fifth Battleship Division, for the duration of World War II.

While the decisive Battle of the Atlantic raged, however, she played a much more important role. Vice Admiral Royal E. Ingersoll assumed command of the Atlantic Fleet after King's appointment as Chief of Naval Operations. On 19 January 1942 Ingersoll transferred his staff and three star flag from the heavy cruiser USS *Augusta* to *Constellation*. Ingersoll had received word that the German battleship *Tirpitz* had slipped out into the Atlantic. It was imperative that *Augusta* put to sea as an operational warship without the burden associated with the functions of flagship. On 1 July of the same year, following his promotion, Admiral Ingersoll hoisted his four star flag to the sloop's mizzen top. When the converted gunboat USS *Vixen* was ready for use as flagship, *Constellation* resumed her "standby" role by 20 July. After departing, Ingersoll said in an interview with the *Baltimore Sun*, "Personally, I have never had a more enjoyable time on any ship."[13]

Constellation's skipper during much of World War II was Lieutenant Commander John A. Davis, a retired officer who had been recalled to active duty during the national emergency. He was a fitting choice. Davis was a recipient of the Medal of Honor for heroism as a young Gunners Mate 3d Class during the Spanish-American War.[14]

Following World War II *Constellation* left her berth in Newport for the last time, and was towed to the Boston Navy Yard. There she was placed in ordinary alongside "Old Ironsides," USS *Constitution*. In 1955 *Constellation*, thought by many to be the namesake frigate, was towed to Baltimore in ARD-16, a U.S. Navy floating drydock. The old ship was then presented to the City of Baltimore and a non-profit patriotic organization for restoration and preservation as an historic shrine. After a well-intentioned but misguided attempt to restore her to look like the Baltimore-built 1797 frigate of the same name, *Constellation* became the centerpiece of Baltimore's Inner Harbor in the early 1970s.

Opposite page: USS *Constellation*,
Flagship of the U.S. Atlantic Fleet
January–July 1942. (U.S. Naval
Historical Center)

Vice Admiral Royal Ingersoll
on board his flagship in 1942.
(U.S. Naval Historical Center)

USS *Constellation* leaves floating
dock ARD-16 upon her arrival
in Baltimore in 1955.

U.S. Frigate *Constellation* vs. *L'Isurgente*, 9 February 1799. (By Arthur Disney)

CHAPTER 9

THE LAST LEG

WHILE THE USS *CONSTELLATION* WAS NEVER IN ANY PITCHED naval battles, she was at the center of a controversy surrounding her own history from the late nineteenth to the last decade of the twentieth century. One group of historians, naval architects and others, led by Leon D. Polland, believed that the vessel was the frigate launched in Baltimore in 1797 and subsequently converted and rebuilt as a sloop-of-war in 1854. Their political pull was evident in the Navy's endorsement of their interpretation, and that the ship was "returned" to Baltimore for "restoration." Another school, led largely

USS *Constellation* capturing *Cora* on 25 September 1860. (By Arthur Disney)

by naval architect and maritime historian Howard I. Chapelle, maintained that the frigate was broken up in 1853, and a new sloop-of-war with the same name was launched in 1854 to take its place in the fleet. The Smithsonian Institution presented the unresolved Polland-Chapelle debates in book form as *The Constellation Question* in 1970. By 1991, however, the dispute was effectively ended with the findings of a team at the David Taylor Research Center led by Curator Dana Wegner. Published as *Fouled Anchors: The Constellation Question Answered,* Wegner and his colleagues painstakingly explained the conclusion that the two ships named *Constellation* were very distinct and in no way could have ever been one and the same.

Unfortunately, after some twenty years, the effect of the misguided restoration effort took its toll on the ship's structural integrity. USS *Constellation* was condemned as unsafe by the U.S. Navy and closed to visitors in 1994. The ship's condition had deteriorated to where much of her timber was rotten and a serious "hog" of 38 inches endangered her keel. The ship's rig was removed, and she was closed to the public to await her fate. Baltimore Mayor Kurt L. Schmoke appointed a Blue Ribbon Commission to explore options for saving the vessel. As a result, the Constellation Foundation was launched, and a Board of Directors was appointed to assume the daunting task of restoring this historic ship to her former glory.

On a calm November day in 1996, *Constellation* was gently moved from her berth at the Inner Harbor to a "graving dock," or small dry dock, near Fort McHenry. The metal door, or "caisson," at the mouth of the dock was closed, and the water was pumped out to leave the ship high and dry. Because of her age and the structural changes made over the years, *Constellation*'s bow and stern ends were 38 inches lower than her center. This condition known as a "hog" or "hogging" occurs when the vessel's structure is weakened through deterioration. Being less buoyant at the ends than at the center, the ship began to sag, developing a concave curve in her keel.

The first task of restoration was to straighten the keel, which is the ship's backbone. Although some of the curve was taken out of the keel in the dry docking process, the keel was so severely distorted that the restoration staff feared catastrophic failure had all of the hog been removed at once. After dry docking, the rest of the hog was removed by easing the center down through the incremental, systematic removal of the keel blocking supports that had been built in the dry dock to receive the ship in her hogged condition. When completed, *Constellation*'s keel was straight once more.

Demolition then began on *Constellation*'s spar and gun decks, and approximately two thirds of the hull planking. Some sections of frames, or the ship's ribs, were removed where necessary and replaced with new laminated white oak. The frames could then act as a mold for the new planking system. *Constellation*'s original frames were too old to receive new fastenings and traditional methods would have required replacement of the entire framing structure. The frames were sufficient, however, to support an innovative procedure known as "cold molding." This technique consists of layering laminations of planking over the frames, with each layer glued to the next. The inside and outside layers are laid fore and aft, while the center layers are laid at opposite diagonal angles. The resulting structure is 30 percent stronger than the original and allows for the preservation of approximately 50 percent of *Constellation*'s historic fabric.

The retained old planking and the new spar deck then had to be caulked. Caulking is the process used to make a wooden ship watertight. A strand of cotton fiber is laid into the plank seam and hammered in tightly. Two strands of oakum, a product made of tarred hemp, are then laid on top of the fiber and also hammered in tightly. The seam is then filled in with hot pitch to protect the cotton and oakum from the elements. Once the planking was watertight, the ship was ready to go back in the water.

Constellation was refloated in August 1998, after more than eighteen months in the graving dock. The event marked the halfway point of the restoration effort. Once again afloat, *Constellation* was able to show off her restored hull and beautiful sheer to all those present for the Launch Day festivities.

Constellation's restoration effort took approximately thirty-two months and encompassed many big projects, but the numerous details were not forgotten. Painting, carving, and installing the numerous small parts and effects that give *Constellation* her special personality received plenty of attention, too. These jobs included restoring the billet head and entry port sideboards.

After she was finally ready, USS *Constellation* returned to her place as the queen of Baltimore's Inner Harbor on 2 July 1999. Escorted by Navy and Coast Guard vessels, Army watercraft and the historic steam tug *Baltimore*, she arrived back at Pier 1 (also known as Constellation Dock) to the sounds of martial music played by the U.S. Naval Academy Band. A thundering salute from the 105mm howitzers of a Maryland Army National Guard field artillery battery, and a flyover by two Navy F/A-18 Hornet fighters heralded her arrival. Boats from the Baltimore Police Department's Marine Division circled the sloop-of-war with their blue lights flashing, while the Baltimore Fire Department's fireboat greeted *Constellation* home with a salute from her water cannon. Thousands watched and cheered from the waterfront, nearby skyscrapers, and Federal Hill. Millions more listened by radio, or watched later on television evening news.

Once the ship was secured to Constellation Dock, it was time to officially thank all those who contributed their time, money, and labor to save the historic vessel. Baltimore Mayor Kurt L. Schmoke, Maryland Governor Parris Glendening, and former Secretary of the Navy John H. Dalton led an array of elected officials, community leaders, and other dignitaries in praise of the artisans who completed the task, and the local community for their unwavering support. Constellation Foundation Chairman Gail Shawe proclaimed the work of that body finished, and turned the helm of operation, continued restoration and preservation of the ship over to Living Classrooms Foundation. With the end of the ceremony, USS *Constellation* was once again open to the public: a cherished icon, historic shrine and priceless cultural resource, restored to her proper 1854 appearance.

USS *Constellation* in Naples, circa 1862, by Tomoso de Simone.

USS *Constellation* firing at a Blockade Runner in 1864. (By Arthur Disney)

USS *Constellation* in
dry-dock at the New
York Navy Yard.
(National Archives)

USS *Constellation* at Newport, Rhode Island.

Midshipmen receive instruction on the spar deck of the sloop *Dale*, a smaller training vessel at Annapolis before putting to sea on *Constellation* on her annual training cruise, circa 1879. (U.S. Naval Historical Center)

Constellation "Welcome Home" at
Constellation Dock on 2 July 1999.
(Photo by Bill McAllen)

Opposite page top: Visitors help "crew"
members demonstrate the workings of the
capstan on *Constellation*'s spar deck.

Opposite page bottom: Two visitors get
"a feel for the job" of helmsman during one
of the many programs on board the ship.

In handwriting on image: *Tyrone Power, taken a gangway of U.S.S. Constella used as background for the picture "Crash Dive" Aug. 194*

In August 1942, *Constellation* served as a backdrop at the end of the movie "Crash Dive." Lieutenant Commander Jon A. Davis, *Constellation*'s skipper (left), is seen here with the film's star, Tyrone Power.

USS *Constellation*, December 1904. (U.S. Naval Historical Center)

USS *Constellation* back at Constellation Dock in Baltimore's Inner Harbor. (Photo by Robert Willasch)

Opposite page top: USS *Constellation* undergoing restoration in the graving dock.

Opposite page bottom: After straightening the keel and restoring the hull, *Constellation* waits to be refloated.

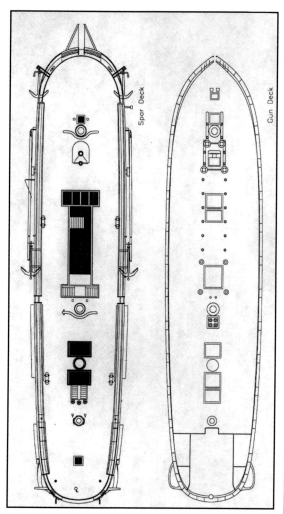

Left diagram: Spar Deck. (A) Forecastle-position of forward pivot gun. (B) Main Hatch (C) Stern-position of the aft pivot gun. Gun Deck. (D) Galley (E) Captain's Cabin

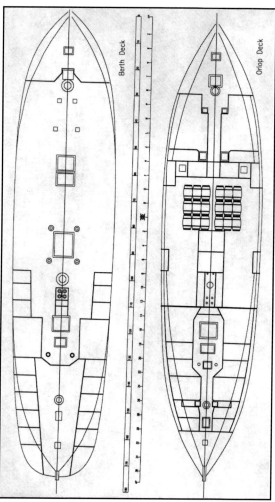

Right diagram: Berth Deck. (F) Sick Bay (G) Crew's Quarters (H) Midshipmen's & Warrant Officers' Quarters (I) Officers' Wardroom Orlop Deck: (J) Forward Orlop (K) Hold (L) Aft Orlop

END NOTES

Chapter 1: The Glorious Namesake.

1. U.S. Navy, Office of Naval Records and Library (hereafter ONR), *Naval Documents Related to the United States Wars with the Barbary Powers* (hereafter Barbary Wars), Volume 1, *Naval Operations, Including Diplomatic Background from 1785 through 1801* (Washington, DC: United States Government Printing Office, 1939), 90–91.

2. Ibid., 75, 122–3.

3. Ibid., 107, 139, 150, 187–8, 244–4.

4. Theodore Roscoe and Fred Freeman, *Picture History of the U.S. Navy: From Old Navy to New, 1776 to 1897* (New York: Bonanza Books, 1956), 264–265.

5. Ibid., 263, 266, 268, 270.

6. ONR, *Naval Documents Related to the Quasi War Between the United States and France* (hereafter *QuasiWar*): *Naval Operations from November 1799 to March 1799* (Washington, DC: United States Government Printing Office, 1935), 326–336.

7. ONR, *Quasi War: Naval Operations from January 1800 to May 1800* (Washington, DC: United States Government Printing Office, 1935), 159–175.

8. ONR, *Barbary Wars*, Volume 1, *Naval Operations, Including Diplomatic Background from 1785-through 1801* (Washington, DC: United States Government Printing Office, 1939), 423–4, 627.

9. Theodore Roosevelt, *The Naval War of 1812* (New York: Modern Library, 1999; previously printed, Annapolis, MD: Naval Institute Press, 1987), 91, 112, 246–8; Roscoe and Freeman, 292–293, 310

10. Naval History Division, *Dictionary of American Naval Fighting Ships*, Volume II, (Washington, DC: Government Printing Office, 1963), 171.

11. Ibid.

12. Dana Wegner, Colin Ratcliff, and Kevin Lynaugh, *Fouled Anchors: The Constellation Question Answered* (Washington, DC: National Technical Information Service and U.S. Government Printing Office, 1991), 3–4.

Chapter 2: The Same Venerable Name

1. Wegner, Ratcliff, and Lynaugh, 3.

2. Ibid., 3–5.

3. Ibid., 4.

4. "The Sloop-of-War Constellation," *Daily Southern Argus* (hereafter *Argus*), Norfolk, VA, Wednesday, 16 August 1854, original in the Marshall W. Butt Library, Portsmouth Naval Shipyard Museum, Portsmouth, VA; and, "U.S. Sloop-of-War Constellation," *Daily Transcript* (hereafter *Transcript*), Portsmouth, VA, Monday, 28 August 1854, original in Huntington Library and Art Gallery, San Marino, CA.

5. "The Old Constellation," *Argus*, 11 July 1853.

6. *Argus*, 28 August 1854.

7. *Transcript*, 28 August 1854.

8. National Archives Records Administration (hereafter NARA),Gosport Store Returns, Returns of Stores at Navy Yards and Naval Stations Records of the Bureau of Ships Entry 320, RG 19.

9. August 1854.

10. NARA, Journal Logbook, Navy Yard, Gosport, Records of Bureau of Yards and Docks RG 71.

11. NARA, Muster Log dated 31 December 1857, RG 24.

12. NARA, Deck Logs, USS *Constellation* 1859–1861, RG 24.

13. William P. Schwartz [alias Samuel P. Ramsey], letter (hereafter, Schwartz letter) to his father, Samuel Schwartz, 4 May 1856, typewritten manuscript (TMs) transcribed by Dr. John F. Schwartz, William's great grandson, and in his possession in Gettysburg, PA. Schwartz used the alias Ramsey to join the Marine Corps in 1851 to conceal his status as a deserter from the U.S. Army in 1849. He died in 1866 while still serving in the marines.

14. NARA, Deck Logs, USS *Constellation* 1859–1861, RG 45.

15. Schwartz, letter to his father dated 3 February 1856.

16. NARA, Letters Received by the Secretary of the Navy from Captains of Ships, RG 45.

17. Schwartz, letter to his brother Charles Schwartz, 8 July 1856.

18. *Constellation* Deck Logs 1859–1861, RG 45.

Chapter 3: Slave Trade Interdiction

1. Warren S. Howard, *American Slavers and the Federal Law 1837–1862* (Los Angeles, CA: University of California Press, 1963), 2-3.

2. Ibid.

3. *United States Statutes at Large*, Vol. I, Sections 1-2 (Boston: Little Brown, 1845–1866) 347–349.

4. Ibid., Volume II, Sections 2–3, 70–71.

5. Ibid., Volume I, Sections 2–3, 451.

6. Ibid., Volume III, Sections 4–5, 690–691.

7. Warren S. Howard, 3–4.

8. Ibid., 14–17.

9. NARA, Letters Received by the Secretary of the Navy from the Captains of Cruisers (hereafter "Squadron Letters"), 1841–1866, File M89, Roll 109, RG 45.

10. James C. Lawrence, Journal of a Cruise amongst the Madeira, Canary, and the Cape Verde Islands, and the West Coast of Africa, 1844 & 45, handwritten manuscript, Special Collections, U.S. Naval Academy Archives, Nimitz Library, Annapolis, MD.

11. NARA, Correspondence of the Secretary of the Navy, Directives (hereafter "Directives"), 1798–1895, Microfilm File Entry (hereafter "File") 42; and 1798-1862, Roll M977, Record Group (hereafter "RG"), 45.

12. Donald L. Canney, *Lincoln's Navy: The Ships, Men and Organization, 1861-1865* (Annapolis, MD: Naval Institute Press, 1998), 17.

13. NARA, Letters Received by the Secretary of the Navy from the Officers Commanding Squadrons (hereafter "Squadron Letters"), 1841–1866, File M89, Roll 109, RG 45.

14. NARA, Muster Rolls, US Navy Ships 1813–1861, File T-829, Roll 2, RG 45.

15. NARA, Armament of Naval Vessels, Volume 1 of 4, 1841–1861, and Squadron Letters, File M89, Roll 109, RG 45.

16. NARA, Squadron Letters, File M89, Roll 112, RG 45; William H. French, interview, "Chasing Slavers with Old Wooden Navy," *Springfield* (Massachusetts) *Daily Republican*, 16 September 1924; and Nathan Miller, *The U.S. Navy: A History*, (Annapolis, MD: Naval Institute Press, 1997), 90.

17. Warren S. Howard, 219-223.

18. NARA, Squadron Letters, File M89, Roll 110, RG 45.

19. NARA, Squadron Letters, File M89, Roll 114, RG 45.

20. French interview.

21 Warren S. Howard, 261.

22. NARA, Squadron Letters, File M89, Roll 114, RG 45.

23. NARA Judiciary Records, US District Court for New York, Southern District, Criminal Docket I, 245, RG O-21.

24. ONR, *Official Record of the Union and Confederate Navies in the War of the Rebellion* (hereafter *Civil War*), Series 1, Volume 1, *Operations of Cruisers January 19, 1861 to December 31, 1862* (Washington, DC: Government Printing Office, 1894), 24; and U.S. Navy Historical Center, *Civil War Naval Chronology 1861 to 1865* (Washington, DC: Government Printing Office, 1971), I–14.

25. NARA, Squadron Letters, File M89, Roll 112, RG 45.

26. NARA, Letters by the Secretary of the Navy to Admirals, Commodores and Captains, Volume 2 April – June 1862, RG 45.

27. NARA, Deck Logs, USS *Constellation* 1859–1861, RG 45; and J. Thomas Scharf, *History of the Confederate States Navy* (New York, NY: Gramercy Books, 1888, reprinted in 1996), 819.

28. David M. Sullivan, *The United States Marine Corps in the Civil War*, Volume I (Shippensburg, PA: White Mane Publishing Co., 1997), ; and, Ralph Donnelly, *The Confederate States Marine Corps: The Rebel Leathernecks* (Shippensburg, PA: White Mane Publishing Co., 1990), 212.

29. William A. Leonard, Diary, handwritten, in the possession of Richard L. Jasse, Ph.D., his great grand son, Rocky Mount, VA; Kevin Conley Ruffin, *Maryland's Blue and Gray: A Border State's Union and Confederate Junior Officer Corps* (Baton Rouge, LA: Louisiana State University Press, 1997), 47.

Chapter 4: Civil War Service

1. Dennis J. Ringle, *Life in Mr. Lincoln's Navy* (Annapolis, MD: Naval Institute Press, 1998), 9.

2. NARA, Muster Roll, USS *Constellation*, 10 March 1862, RG 45; and 1 March 1862, RG 24.

3. Moses A. Safford, "A Man-of-War Man's Diary: A Cruise in an Old Frigate Prefaced by an Autobiography of the Diarist," Diary, Typewritten Manuscript (TMs), edited by Victor Safford, Boston, MA, 1933 (USS *Constellation* Archive Collection, Baltimore, MD), D-114. USS *Cumberland* was an all-wood, all-sail sloop like *Constellation*, sunk by the ironclad CSS *Virginia*, the former *Merrimack*, in 1862.

4. Robert J. Schneller, Jr., *A Quest for Glory: A Biography of Rear Admiral John A. Dahlgren* (Annapolis, MD: Naval Institute Press, 1996), 227.

5. NARA, Yards and Docks Returns, Report of Services, 10 March 1862, RG 71.

6. Safford, D-13. Ironically, Raphael Semmes had served on the frigate *Constellation* as a Passed Midshipman and Master.

7. Charles F. Blake, Journal 1862–1864, TMs, transcribed by Eleanor Cabot Lyford, his granddaughter (U.S. Naval Historical Center Library, Washington, DC), 6.

8. ONR, *Civil War*, Series 1, Volume 1, *Operations of Cruisers January 19, 1861 to December 31, 1862* (Washington, DC: Government Printing Office, 1894), 381.

9. Ibid., Series I, Volume II, 371-2.

10. NARA, Captains' Letters, Volume II, E–37, 57, RG 45.

11. Ibid., Volume II, E–37, 257, RG 45.

12. Safford, D–311.

13. NARA, Captain's Letters, Volume II, E–37, 226, RG 45.

14. Ibid., 195.

15. Ibid., 226.

16. Safford, D–317.

17. NARA, Captains' Letters, Volume II, E–37, 262, RG 45.

18. Ibid., 266.

Chapter 5: Uncle Sam's Web Feet

1. Dennis J. Ringle, *Life in Mr. Lincoln's Navy* (Annapolis, MD: Naval Institute Press, 1889), 9; Harold D. Langley, "The Sailor's Life," *Images of War*, Volume I, *Fighting for Time*, William C. Davis, ed. (Garden City, NY: Doubleday, 1981), 361–2. The term "Jack Tar" combined 'Jack,' or workman, with 'tar,' the substance used for waterproofing sailors' clothing. It was akin to calling soldiers of the U.S. Army "G.I. Joe" in WWII.

2. NARA, USS *Constellation* Muster Roll dated 1 March 1863, Muster Rolls, U.S. Navy Ships 1862–1865, RG 24; Francis Trevelyan Miller, ed., *The Photographic History of the Civil War* in Ten Volumes, Part 6, *The Navies* (New York, NY: Castle Books, 1911, reprinted in 1957), 282; Ringle, 41–2.

3. Commodore Chas. S. McCauley and Commander G. S. Blake, USN, *Tables of Allowances of Equipment, Outfits, Stores &c., for the Vessels in the Navy of the United States* (Washington, DC: A.O.P Nicholson, 1854), 192–4; NARA, USS *Constellation* Muster Roll dated 10 March 1862, RG 24; Safford Diary, B-29–30; Francis Trevelyan

Miller, 282–4.

4. Ibid.

5. Safford Diary, B-30; NARA, *Constellation* Muster Roll dated 10 March 1862, RG 24; Ringle, 40.

6. NARA, USS *Constellation* Muster Roll dated 10 March 1862, RG 24; Ringle, 12–13.

7. NARA, USS *Constellation* Muster Roll dated 10 March 1862, and 1 March 1863, RG 24; Safford, D-7; Ringle 13-14. It was once generally believed that black sailors made up as much as 20% of the Navy's lower enlisted strength. Recent study by Professor Joseph P. Reidy at Howard University has revised this estimate down to about 10 percent.

8. NARA, USS *Constellation* Muster Roll dated 10 March 1862, RG 24; McCauley and Blake, 193–4; Timothy Whelan (alias Wayland), Diary (in the possession of Catherine Peters, his great granddaughter), Martha's Vineyard, MA; Ford was promoted to First Lieutenant in 1864. Whelan used the alias to avoid anti-Irish discrimination. He later corrected the records to show his proper name.

9. Schwartz letter to his brother Charles, 8 July 1856; Department of the Navy *Ordnance Instructions for the United States Navy Relating to the Preparation of Vessels of War for Battle* (hereafter *Ordnance Instructions*) (Washington, DC: George W. Bowman, 1860), 15, xxi, xxiv.

10. Safford, D–18.

11. Schwartz letter to his brother Charles, 8 July 8, 1856; Francis Lord, *They Fought for the Union* (New York, NY: Bonanza Books, 1980), 300.

12. McCauley and Blake, 193–4; Canney, 101-2; .

13. McCauley and Blake, 193; Lord, 538-9; Canney, 141–150.

14. McCauley and Blake, 193; Lord, 538-9; Canney, 141–150; Blake, 1; James Russell Soley *Historical Sketch of the United States Naval Academy* (Washington, DC: Government Printing Office, 1876), 101–2.

15. NARA, Captains Letters, E–37, 22, 262, RG 45.

16. NARA, Captains Letters, E–37, 57, RG 45; Safford, D–121; Canney, 145.

Chapter 6: Life on a Man-of-War

1. Canney, 122–3; Ringle, 27.

2. Safford, D–137.

3. Safford, D–130.

4. Canney, 128–30; Ringle, 41–2.

5. Ibid.; Blake, 1.

6. Canney, 128; McCauley and Blake, 192; *Ordnance Instructions*, xii.

7. Blake, 2–3.

8. Safford, D-77.

9. McCauley and Blake, 192–3; Ringle, 73.

10. Canney, 130; Ringle, 74; Safford, D–107.

11. Safford, D–5, 34.

12. McCauley and Blake, 191–2; Ringle, 111–3; Safford, D–79.

13. Safford, D–39.

14. *Ordnance Instructions*, 32.

15. Safford, D–103.

16. Ibid., D–112.

17. Ibid., D–75.

18. Ringle, 89–90; Safford, D–3, D–92.

19. McCauley and Blake, 191; Ringle, 89; Safford, D–80, 125).

20. Canney, 126–7; Ringle, 104 .

21. Safford, D–25.

22. Canney, 126–7; Ringle, 102–104.

23. Safford, D–165.

24. Ibid., D–174.

25. Ibid., D–175.

26. Canney, 136–7; Ringle, 84; Safford, D–113.

27. Blake, 3.

28. NARA, Recruiting Posters, US Navy 1863 and US Marine Corps 1866, Photograph and Print Collection; Safford, D–24.

29. Blake, 11.

30. Safford, D–126.

31. Safford, D–55.

32. Blake, 10. "Miss L." was Mary Ladd, daughter of Eliphalet Ladd, of Portsmouth, New Hampshire, who later became Blake's wife.

Chapter 7: Fighting on a Man-of-War

1. Safford, D–10.

2. *Ordnance Instructions*, 3–6.

3. Blake, 1.

4. Safford, D–36.

5. Blake, 6.

6. *Ordnance Instructions*, 3; Safford, D–12, 90.

7. NARA, Record of Services, 10 March 1862, Bureau of Ships, RG 45; Edwin Olmstead, Wayne C. Stark, and Spencer Tucker, *The Big Guns: Civil War Siege, Seacoast and Naval Cannon* (Bloomfield, Ontario: Museum Restoration Service, 1997), 38–48.

8. *Ordnance Instructions*, 22, 23, 57, 58.

9. *A Treatise on Ordnance and Naval Gunnery, Compiled and Arranged as a Text Book for the U.S. Naval Academy* (New York, NY: D. Van Nostrand, 1862), 137–142; Olmstead, Stark, and Tucker, 113–115, *Ordnance Instruction*, 68, xx.

10. Olmstead, Stark, and Tucker, 103–7; *Ordnance Instruction*, 77–78.

11. *Ordnance Instruction*, 9, 15, 27–28, xxii.

12. Ibid, 15, 29–30, xxiii, xxiv.

13. Ibid, 12, 15, 29–31, xxiv.

14. Ibid, 14, 27, 32, 93, xxiv.
15. Ibid, 15, 79, xxiv.
16. Ibid, 5, 19, 21–24, 26, 38, 77–79, 160.
17. Ibid, 38, 38, 78.
18. Ibid, 20, 39.
19. Safford, D–119.
20. Ibid, D–125.

Chapter 8: Practice and Training Ship

1. NARA, Returns of the Norfolk Navy Yard 1874, RG 71; Deck Log USS *Constellation* June to September 1871, RG 45.
2. NARA, Returns for 1874, Bureau of Construction and Repair, RG 19.
3. Herbert O. Dunn, Notebook, Handwritten, 1874, in the collection of USS *Constellation* Museum, Baltimore, MD.
4. Conduct Book, Class of 1879, U.S. Naval Academy Archives, Special Collections, Admiral Chester W. Nimitz Library, Annapolis, MD; William B. Cogar, *Dictionary of Admirals of the U.S. Navy*, Volume 2, 1901–1918, Annapolis, MD: Naval Institute Press, 1996), 76–77.
5. NARA, Deck Log USS *Constellation* 18 March to 2 September 1880, RG 45.
6. Original Proclamation, Copy from the personal papers of Captain Edward E. Potter, in the possession of Edward Potter Sabin, his grandson, Ellicott City, MD.
7. NARA, USS *Constellation* Deck Log 1 June 1893 to 2 September 1893, RG 45.
8. Roscoe and Freeman, 961, 968–9.
9. NARA, Board of Survey Report from New York Navy Yard 11 July 1904, Bureau of Construction, Box 1260, RG 19.
10. Letter from F. D. Roosevelt, Acting Secretary of the Navy to Bureau of Construction and Repair, 16 June 1913, RG 45.
11. Memo, Navy Department to Bureau of construction, 2 May 1915, RG 19.
12. Letter, Commanding Officer Newport Naval Training Center to Bureau of Construction and Repair, 8 February 1926, RG 19.
13. E. T. Baker, "Ingersoll of the Atlantic Fleet," *Baltimore Sun*, 28 February 1943; Letter to author from John R. Norris, veteran, 1999, Collection of USS *Constellation* Museum.
14. Donald E. Cooke, *For Conspicuous Gallantry: Winners of the Medal of Honor* (Maplewood, NJ: C. S. Hammond and Co., 1966), 74.

BIBLIOGRAPHY

Unpublished Personal Diaries and Letters:

Charles F. Blake (Midshipman, USN), "Journal of Charles F. Blake 1862–1864," diary, typewritten manuscript (TMs) transcribed by Mrs. Frederick Lyford (nee Eleanor Cabot), his granddaughter. Located in Special Collections, Navy Library, U.S. Naval Historical Center, Washington Navy Yard, Washington, D.C.

John M. Brown (Fleet Surgeon, USN), letter, handwritten, to his sister Emma, 12 January 1861. Located in the collection of USS Constellation Museum, Baltimore, MD.

Herbert O. Dunn (Cadet Midshipman, USN), "Seamanship" notebook 1874, handwritten. Located in the collection of USS Constellation Museum, Baltimore, MD.

James C. Lawrence (Master's Mate, USN), "Journal of a Cruise amongst the Madeira, Canary, and the Cape Verde Islands, and the West Coast of Africa, 1844 & 45," handwritten, and typewritten manuscript (TMs). Located in Special Collections, U.S. Naval Academy Archives, Chester W. Nimitz Library, Annapolis, MD.

William A. Leonard (Ordinary Seaman, USN), diary 1859–1861, handwritten, in the possession of Richard L. Jasse, his great-grandson, Rocky Mount, VA.

Moses A. Safford (Yeoman, USN), "A Man-of-War's Man's Diary: A Cruise in an Old Frigate Prefaced by an Autobiography of the Diarist," diary 1862–1865, typewritten manuscript (TMs), edited and transcribed by Victor Safford, Boston, MA 1933. Located in USS Constellation Museum Collection, Baltimore, MD.

William P. Schwartz [alias Samuel P. Ramsey] (Orderly Sergeant, USMC), letters to his family 1855–1858, and diary, 1855–1858, handwritten, transcribed by Dr. John F. Schwartz, his great-grandson, and in his possession, Gettysburg, PA.

Timothy Whelan [alias Wayland] (Sergeant, USMC), diary 1862–1865, handwritten, in possession of Catherine Peters, his great-granddaughter, Martha's Vinyard, MA.

Government Documents:

National Archives and Records Administration (NARA), Old Navy Records:
Lists of Officers on Vessels 1834–1865, Entry 181, Record Group (RG) 24.

Muster Rolls, U.S. Navy Ships 1862–1865, RG 24.

Muster Rolls, U.S. Navy Ships 1813–1861, Microfilm T–829, Roll 2, RG 45.

Lists of Officers on Vessels 1861–1877, Entry 96, RG 45.

Correspondence of the Secretary of the Navy, Directives, 1798–1895 Microfilm File, Entry 42; and 1798–1862, Entry M977, RG 45.

Letters Received by the Secretary of the Navy from Commanding Officers of Squadrons ("Squadron Letters"), 1841–1866, Microfilm File M89, RG 45.

Letters of Rear Admirals, Commodores and Captains to the Secretary of the Navy, 1862–1866 ("Captains' Letters"), Volumes I and II, Entry 37, RG 45.

Letters of Rear Admirals, Commodores and Captains to the Secretary of the Navy, 1805–1862, Microfilm File M125, RG 45.

Deck Logs, USS Constellation 1855–1893, RG 45.

Records of the Bureau of Construction and Repair of, RG 19.

Records of the Bureau of Yards and Docks, RG 71.

Records of the Bureau of Ordnance, RG 74.

Northeast Regional Archives, Judiciary Records:

Records of U.S. District Court for New York, Southern District, Criminal Docket, RG O-21.

Published Sources:

E. T. Baker, "Ingersoll of the Atlantic Fleet," *Baltimore Sun*, 28 February 1943. Located in USS Constellation Museum Collection, Baltimore, MD.

Donald L. Canney, <u>Lincoln's Navy: The Ships, Men and Organization, 1861–1865</u>, Annapolis, MD: Naval Institute Press, 1998.

Howard I. Chapelle and Leon D. Polland, <u>The Constellation Question</u>, Washington, DC: Smithsonian Institution Press, 1970.

William B. Cogar, <u>Dictionary of Admirals of the U.S. Navy</u>, Volumes I and II, Annapolis, MD: Naval Institute Press, 1996.

Donald E. Cooke, <u>For Conspicuous Gallantry: Winners of the Medal of Honor</u>, Maplewood, NJ: C. S. Hammond and Co., 1966.

The People of the City and County of Cork, Ireland, Proclamation of Thanks, 1880, Copy from the personal papers of Captain Edward E. Potter, in the possession of Edward Potter Sabin, his grandson, Ellicott City, MD.

Ralph Donnelly, <u>The Confederate States Marine Corps: The Rebel Leathernecks</u>, Shippensburg, PA: White Mane Publishing Co., 1990.

William French (Interview), "Chasing Slavers with Old Wooden Navy," *Springfield* (Massachusetts) *Daily Republican*, 16 September 1924. Original clippings preserved and maintained by Beverly M. Martinoli, his great-granddaughter, in Oxford, CT.

William H. French (Interview), "City's Oldest Adventurer Seeks Post on Battle Scarred Warship,' *Springfield Union*, 27 July 1926. Microfilm copy located in the Springfield Valley Historical Museum Library, Springfield, MA.

"At the Gosport Navy Yard," *Daily Southern Argus*, Norfolk, VA, 28 August 1854. Original located in the Marshall W. Butt Library, Portsmouth Naval Shipyard Museum, Portsmouth, VA.

"At the Gosport Navy Yard," *Daily Transcript*, Portsmouth, VA, 28 August 1854. Original located in the Marshall W. Butt Library, Portsmouth Naval Shipyard Museum, Portsmouth, VA.

Warren S. Howard, <u>American Slavers and the Federal Law 1837–1862</u>, Los Angeles, CA: University of California Press, 1963.

Calvin Lane, "The African Squadron: The U.S. Navy and the Slave Trade, 1820–1862," *The Log of Mystic Seaport*, Volume 50, No. 4, Spring 1999.

Harold D. Langley, "The Sailor's Life," Images of War, Volume I, Fighting for Time, William C. Davis, ed., Garden City, NY: Doubleday, 1981.

Francis Lord, They Fought for the Union, New York, NY: Bonanza Books, 1980.

Commodore Charles S. McCauley and Commander G. S. Blake, U.S. Navy, Tables of Allowances of Equipment, Outfits, Stores etc., for the Vessels in the Navy of the United States, Washington DC: A. O. P. Nicholson, Public Printer, 1854. NARA, RG 45.

Francis Trevelyan Miller, ed., The Photographic History of the Civil War in Ten Volumes, Part 6, The Navies, New York, NY: Castle Books, 1906, reprinted in 1957.

Nathan Miller, The U.S. Navy, A History, Annapolis, MD: Naval Institute Press, 1997.

"The Old Constellation," Daily Southern Argus, Norfolk, VA, 11 July 1853. Located in the Marshall W. Butt Library, Portsmouth Naval Shipyard Museum, Portsmouth, VA.

Edwin Olmstead, Wayne C. Stark, and Spencer Tucker, The Big Guns: Civil War Siege, Seacoast and Naval Cannon, Bloomfield, Ontario: Museum Restoration Service, 1997.

Admiral David Dixon Porter, U.S.N., The Naval History of the Civil War, New York, NY: Sherman Publishing Co., 1886, reprinted, Mineola, NY: Dover Publications, 1998.

Dennis J. Ringle, Life in Mr. Lincoln's Navy, Annapolis, MD: Naval Institute Press, 1998.

Theodore Roscoe and Fred Freeman, Picture History of the U.S. Navy: From Old Navy to New, 1776 to 1897, New York, NY: Bonanza Books, 1956.

J. Thomas Scharf, History of the Confederate States Navy: From Its Organization to the Surrender of Its Last Vessel, New York, NY: Gramercy Books, 1887, reprinted in 1996.

Robert J. Schneller, Jr., A Quest for Glory: A Biography of Rear Admiral John A. Dahlgren, Annapolis, MD: Naval Institute Press, 1996.

Edward Simpson, Lieutenant, U.S. Navy, A Treatise on Ordnance and Naval Gunnery, Compiled and Arranged as a Text Book for the U.S. Naval Academy, New York, NY: D. Van Nostrand, Public Printers, 1862. Located in Navy Library, Rare Book Collection, U.S. Navy Historical Center, Washington Navy Yard, Washington, DC.

"The Sloop-of-War Constellation," *Daily Southern Argus*, Norfolk, VA, Wednesday, 16 August 1854. Located in the Marshall W. Butt Library, Portsmouth Naval Shipyard Museum, Portsmouth, VA.

James Russell Soley, Historical Sketch of the United States Naval Academy, Washington, DC: Government Printing Office, 1876. Located in Special Collections, U.S. Naval Academy Archives, Nimitz Library, Annapolis, MD.

David M. Sullivan, The United States Marine Corps in the Civil War (Three Volumes), Shippensburg, PA: White Mane Publishing Co., 1997.

Hugh Thomas, The Slave Trade: The Story of the Atlantic Slave Trade: 1440–1870, New York, NY: Simon and Schuster, 1997.

U.S. Navy Department, Naval History Division, Civil War Naval Chronology 1861–1865, Washington, DC: Government Printing Office, 1971.

U.S. Navy Department, Naval History Division, Dictionary of American Naval Fighting Ships, Volume II, Washington, DC: Government Printing Office, 1963.

U.S. Navy Department, Office of Naval Records and Library, Naval Documents Related to the United States Wars with the Barbary Powers, Volume 1, Naval Operations, Including Diplomatic Background from 1785 through 1801, Washington, DC: Government Printing Office, 1939.

U.S. Navy Department, Office of Naval Records and Library, Naval Documents Related to the Quasi War Between the United States and France: Naval Operations from November 1799 to March 1799; Washington, DC: Government Printing Office, 1935.

U.S. Navy Department, Office of Naval Records and Library, Naval Documents Related to the Quasi War Between the United States and France: Naval Operations from January 1800 to May 1800, Washington, DC: Government Printing Office, 1935.

U.S. Navy Department, Office of Navy Records, Official Records of the Union and Confederate Navies in the War of the Rebellion, Series 1, Volume 1, Operations of Cruisers January 19, 1861 to December 31, 1862, Washington, DC: Government Printing Office, 1894.

U.S. Navy Department, Ordnance Instructions for the United States Navy, Relating to the Preparation of Vessels of War for Battle: to the Duties of Officers and Others When at Quarters: to Ordnance and Ordnance Stores, and to Gunnery, Second Edition,

Washington, DC: George W. Bowman, Public Printer, 1860. NARA, RG 45.

U.S. Navy Department, <u>Ordnance Instruction for the United States Navy</u>, Washington, DC: Government Printing Office, 1866. Located in USS Constellation Museum Collection, Baltimore, MD.

"U.S. Sloop-of-War Constellation," *Daily Transcript*, Portsmouth, VA, Monday, 28 August 1854. Located in Huntington Library and Art Gallery, San Marino, CA.

<u>United States Statutes at Large</u>, Vol. I–III, Boston, MA: Little Brown, 1845–1866.

Dana Wegner, Colin Ratcliff, and Kevin Lynaugh, <u>Fouled Anchors: The Constellation Question Answered</u>, Washington, DC: National Technical Information Service and U.S. Government Printing Office, 1991.

ABOUT THE AUTHOR

GLENN F. WILLIAMS IS A RETIRED MILITARY OFFICER WHO HAS also been a "public historian" since he was in high school. He began as a sixteen-year-old naval cadet and docent on board USS *Constellation* in 1969, when it was generally believed she was the frigate launched at Baltimore in 1797. After earning a BA degree in History from Loyola College in 1975 and working as a seasonal park ranger at Fort McHenry National Monument and Historic Shrine, he was commissioned as an Infantry officer through the U.S. Army Reserve Officer Training Corps. Throughout more than twenty years of service, in addition to his primary assignments, he was frequently given the additional duty of historian for the organizations to which he belonged, taught military history in both formal and informal training courses, and volunteered at museums and historic sites in his "off-duty" time. Following retirement from the Army and over two years' experience with a government contractor, he returned to a full-time public history career as the Assistant Curator at the Baltimore Civil War Museum before accepting his current position as Historian and Curator of Exhibits for the USS *Constellation* Museum in 1999.

In addition to completing a MA degree in Advanced Historical Studies, Public History track, at University of Maryland Baltimore County, he holds a MA in Human Resources Development from Webster University, is a graduate of the U.S. Army Command and General Staff College, and is the author of several articles on military and naval history.

Glenn met his wife Patricia while working aboard *Constellation* in 1971. They have been married for more than twenty-five years, and make their home in Catonsville, Maryland. They have three sons, Glenn Jr., Michael, and Edward, of whom they are most proud.

ACKNOWLEDGMENTS

I AM GRATEFUL FOR THE ASSISTANCE AND COOPERATION SHOWED TO me by staffs at the U.S. Naval Historical Center, U.S. Marine Corps Historical Center, U.S. Naval Academy Archives; National Archives Old Navy Records in Washington, D.C., Cartographic Records in College Park, Maryland, and Judiciary Records, Northeast Region, in New York, New York; U.S. Library of Congress; U.S. Army Military History Institute at Carlisle Barracks, Pennsylvania; the Marshall W. Butt Portsmouth Naval Shipyard Museum and Library in Portsmouth, Virginia; the Springfield Valley Historical Museum Library, Springfield, Massachusetts; Kittery Historic and Naval Museum, Kittery, Maine; Independence Seaport Museum, Philadelphia, Pennsylvania; and Maryland Historical Society in Baltimore, Maryland.

Deserving of thanks and credit are the many veterans who served on board *Constellation* during her last years on the Navy list who were willing to share their personal recollections: especially John R. Norris, C. Snowden Arthur, and Bruce L. Kubert, to name but a very few. I am also grateful to the many descendants of crew members who contacted me to offer diaries, letters (or excerpts), photographs and other memorabilia from different periods of the ship's history that provided unique first person accounts: especially Dr. John Schwartz, Beverly Martinoli, Dr. Richard Jasse, Catherine Peters, Mimi Long, Edward P. Sabin, Kathleen and Margaret Shinners, and Alice Nagel. Among this group, I include Joseph Frost of the Maine Chapter of the Patriots and Founders of America for records related to Yeoman Moses Safford.

I wish to express my sincere appreciation to Executive Director Christopher Rowsom and the rest of my colleagues and coworkers who I am proud to call friends, as well as all the staff and volunteers of USS *Constellation* Museum. Of particular note are: Holly Burnham, Museum Programs Manager, and her crew of docents and interpreters who help the history of the ship come to life; Paul Powichrowski, Restoration Manager, and his crew for their knowledge of the ship's structural history and their dedication to its historic preservation; Stephanie Linebaugh and her associates in our Education Department who skillfully integrate the ship's history into interdisciplinary learning experiences; Audrey Morsberger and Joe Fales and the staff in the Ship's Store; Jennifer Heimbach, who keeps us all straight administratively; volunteer historian John Barnard; and Larry Bopp, Steve Bockmiller and the rest of Ship's Company, Inc., our "living history" volunteer contingent. All were helpful with advice, constructive criticism, fact checking and proof reading. Accept my deepest apologies for anyone who was unintentionally omitted.

Most of all, I thank the sailors, marines and officers who served aboard USS *Constellation* in peace and war for their service to our country. The preservation of the ship is the preservation of their legacy, and that of their comrades on other ships and stations.